PEARLS *from the* PLATES

Pearls *from the* Plates

Reading and Responding to the Book of Mormon

Karl W. Nehring

CFI
Springville, Utah

ISBN 13: 978-1-59955-246-0

Published by CFI, an imprint of Cedar Fort, Inc., 2373 W. 700 S., Springville, UT 84663
Distributed by Cedar Fort, Inc., www.cedarfort.com

LIBRARY OF CONGRESS CATALOGING-IN-PUBLICATION DATA

Nehring, Karl W., 1949-
Pearls from the plates: Reading and responding to the Book of Mormon / Karl Nehring.
p. cm.
ISBN 978-1-59955-246-0
1. Book of Mormon--Criticism, interpretation, etc. I. Title.

BX8627.N42 2009
289.3'22--dc22

2008048878

Cover design by Jen Boss
Cover design © 2009 by Lyle Mortimer
Edited and typeset by Melissa J. Caldwell

Printed in the United States of America

10 9 8 7 6 5 4 3 2 1

Printed on acid-free paper

Dedicated in loving memory to the late Glenn L. Pearson,
whose love of the Book of Mormon ignited mine.

Contents

Foreword

In his introduction, Karl Nehring describes his book as a response rather than a commentary, and he is right. There are scholarly commentaries on the Book of Mormon. They help us understand this or that point of language, history, or doctrine better so that we will understand its teachings better. Their contribution to our intellect is important. They have an important place in Latter-day Saint literature.

In contrast, Brother Nehring's book shares his response to the Book of Mormon, helping us to respond with our heart, might, and soul, as well as with our mind, by allowing us to participate in the wholeness of his response. He does not think about his reading and then show us the results of that thinking. Instead, Brother Nehring takes us along with him as he reads, as he is surprised or puzzled or amazed by something, and as he thinks about his surprise, puzzlement, and amazement. We discover many things as we read along with him, but what we discover most of all is not a particular content. It is obvious that were we to read the same passages with Brother Nehring again some other time, we would be surprised by them and learn new things, as well. So, though we learn interesting things as we read along with him, things for our own benefit, things we can teach in lessons or talks, the most important thing we learn is a love for the Book of Mormon and a way of continuing to read it over and over again.

Because it helps us learn to read the Book of Mormon and to contemplate its teachings, both first-time and repeat readers of that book will find this book fruitful. Joining Brother Nehring's explorations will help beginners—those as yet outside the Church as well as those in the Church but still young in the gospel—come to a testimony of the Book of Mormon. But *Pearls from the Plates: Reading and Responding to the Book of Mormon* is not only for beginners. Veteran readers will strengthen their testimony of the Book of Mormon by learning a way of reading and rereading that makes it a continually renewing spiritual experience.

Pearls from the Plates is an important contribution to our gospel libraries. It should take its place beside our scriptural commentaries and scholarly works. We should hope that it will be joined by others written in a similar way.

James E. Faulconer
Professor of Philosophy
Brigham Young University
Provo, Utah

Acknowledgments

It would be an impossible task to thank everyone who participated in making this book possible. Over the years I have sat through countless Sunday School lessons, read countless books and articles, listened to countless General conference talks, and engaged in countless discussions with others about the Book of Mormon. The ideas generated in those encounters have no doubt influenced my thoughts about the Book of Mormon and thus helped to shape this book.

Still, it is certainly both possible and imperative to acknowledge the help of those who have contributed meaningfully and generously to this effort. Jim Faulconer of BYU and Scott Burton of CES read manuscript versions and offered both much-needed advice and much-appreciated encouragement. Both of these fine gentlemen are much busier than I am; that they would be willing to take the time to read and comment on what I sent them is simply amazing. I am humbled by their generosity.

Derrick and Tammi Wiemer have no idea that they had anything to do with this book, but their blessings and hugs helped sustain me through some difficult times and made it possible for me to press forward in writing it. I am humbled by their kindness.

I would also like to acknowledge the good folks at Cedar Fort, including Jeffrey Marsh, Heather Holm, and especially Melissa Caldwell, my delightfully deft editor, whose labors have made this book—and this dream—possible. I am sure there are others whose names I unfortunately do not know, but I thank them, too. I am humbled by their diligence

Finally, I must thank Marilyn, my eternal companion. She has encouraged me to keep at it, has given me feedback, and has always been kind to me, even when I have not deserved it. She is a living example of the faith, hope, and charity taught in the Book of Mormon. I am humbled by her love.

Introduction

On Easter Sunday 2005, I was released as a bishop after serving for a little more than five years. For the first few days after my release, I was in a bit of a daze. After a few weeks, I became slightly depressed. It was not that I still wanted to be the bishop, or that I missed the power of the office; rather, it was like being thrust into a vacuum. After five years of always having something to do or someone to worry about, and always thinking about how to solve problems, I suddenly felt adrift.

Until I was released, I had not realized how much my outlook on things had been shaped by my calling as bishop. I had been living on a kind of spiritual adrenaline that was no longer there, and I was suffering from withdrawal symptoms.

Oh, I had a new calling as a member of the stake high council, but that calling did not stimulate the adrenaline in the same way. It was just a calling. Although I tried to adjust to my new routine, and although there were things about my new calling that I looked forward to, I still felt adrift.

After a few more weeks, however, I started to feel better, and decided that I must be getting over my release. A couple of friends who had served as bishops mentioned to me that the hardest part for them had been about six months after their release, but I dismissed this idea as something that must have been peculiar to their experiences. It was certainly not the sort of thing that would happen to me. As another month or two passed by, I started adjusting to my new calling on the high council and quietly rejoicing in the realization that I was now finally over the shock of my release.

Later that summer, though, about five months after my release, I began to realize that something was wrong. I did not feel rebellious, I was not doing anything that I should not have been doing, but I just did not feel right spiritually. My prayers were more perfunctory, my study was more sporadic, and my overall outlook was sliding toward cynicism. Although I did not have much energy, I began to find it harder to sleep. It eventually got to the point that I had to call my doctor to see about getting some sleep medication to help me through my restless nights.

I suddenly realized that I was depressed, that the root of my depression was my release, and that I needed to get over this once and for all and get on with my life. However, realizing what was going on and recognizing that I needed to get over it did nothing to make me actually feel better. If anything, realizing that I was depressed made me feel more depressed. I could feel myself being drawn into an emotional whirlpool from which I felt increasingly unable to escape.

The one bright spot that I saw in my life at that time was our vacation—we had been planning to attend the college graduations of our two older daughters, the blessing of our newest granddaughter, and Education Week at BYU. I hoped that going on this trip would help me get over my feeling of despair—at least for a while.

At about the same time, something else happened. President Gordon B. Hinckley issued a challenge to members of the Church to read or reread the Book of Mormon by the end of the year. As I now look back on this event, I am not sure how I first heard of it. It may have been on an LDS-related website, or maybe I heard it in a stake meeting, or possibly from the pulpit in a church meeting. My home teachers also told me about it, and when my copy of the *Ensign* arrived, I read the challenge for myself.

As we packed our bags for our vacation trip, my intention was to pack my scriptures in one of the big suitcases that we would use as checked baggage. At the last minute, however, I decided that I needed to pack them in my carry-on bag, because I was beginning to get the nagging feeling that I needed to follow President Hinckley's counsel as soon as possible.

As I boarded the plane and got to my seat, I was dismayed to find that I had been assigned to a seat without a window. The plane itself was a small prop plane that was loud, cramped, and uncomfortable. I sat there in my tight little seat for a few minutes, wondering what I should do to pass the time when the thought came to me more and more insistently that I really needed to read the Book of Mormon. In fact, it suddenly became clear to me that I needed to read the Book of Mormon not just by the end of the year, as President Hinckley had counseled, but by the end of my vacation.

I wish I could report that this impression immediately brought me great joy, but to be honest, in some ways this impression felt at first more like another burden rather than a blessing. Still, I knew deep down inside that I really needed to do something to dispel the gloom that had befallen me. I had the distinct impression that reading the Book of Mormon would be beneficial to me, even if I really did not have all that much enthusiasm. Thus I began to read, more from a sense of duty than from any nobler motive.

As the noisy, buzzing, bumping plane finally struggled into the air, I was already drifting away into another world. I had made up my mind that my main goal was simply to read the Book of Mormon, not to study it; that could come later. For now, I just wanted to immerse myself in it and make it through to the end before I finished my vacation.

As the plane droned on toward Detroit, I found myself pressing on toward the promised land with Lehi and his family. I kept turning the pages of the Book of Mormon, becoming thoroughly absorbed in both the story and the teachings found therein.

By the time the little plane was ready to start its final descent toward the runway in Detroit, I had made it through something like seventy-five pages. As I noticed that we were getting ready to land, I also noticed that I had completely forgotten about being depressed.

As I zipped the cover closed on my scriptures, I felt inspired to thank the Lord for both the Book of Mormon and the desire He had given me to read it. Sitting upright in that cramped seat on that noisy plane, I closed my eyes, bowed my head, and poured out my heart to the Lord.

As I finished my brief but earnest prayer, I was overcome by an intense but welcome feeling of peace and relaxation, as though a great burden had been lifted from me. I then had a distinct impression—not quite a voice, but a distinct impression of actual words, a still, small voice cutting through the noisy din of the crowded cabin to tell me with perfect clarity that I was still a High priest and the Lord still had work for me to do. In an instant, I knew that I would no longer feel depressed. I was now ready, able, and willing to move on with my life.

What joy filled my soul! By doing what the prophet had commanded me to do, even though I did it grudgingly at first, I had put myself in a position to receive much-needed personal revelation. I had not even finished the Book of Mormon, and already President Hinckley's promise was being fulfilled.

Over the next week, I kept plugging away at my reading, often staying up late in my room at Deseret Towers while my wife slept. When we boarded the plane in Salt Lake City to head back to Ohio, I still had plenty of reading to do, but I was confident that if I kept at it during the long flight, I could reach my goal.

Wonderfully enough, as the plane carrying me back home started its final approach to the runway, I was able to complete my reading of the Book of Mormon. That evening, I phoned my bishop to let him know I had completed the assignment. Good bishop that he is, he did not cut me any slack; in fact, he immediately counseled me to read the Book of Mormon again, this time more slowly and studiously.

I agreed that this would be a good idea, and so I began reading the Book of Mormon again, this time with an eye toward teaching it, as I had been offered the opportunity to teach an Institute class in the fall. I had not been sure what course I wanted to teach, but now it seemed perfectly and joyfully obvious to me that what I wanted to teach was the Book of Mormon.

As I read the Book of Mormon this second time, I did so a bit more slowly and studiously. At this less frenetic pace, I began to discover things in the Book of Mormon that I had not seen in any of my previous readings, causing me to look forward eagerly to the opportunity of sharing my discoveries with my students.

But as I began to think more seriously about my forthcoming opportunity to teach the Book of Mormon, pesky questions began to pester my mind. What would I teach? What would be my approach? What resources would I draw upon? What would I cover, and what would I have to skip over in the interest of time?

Pondering these questions, I began to read the Book of Mormon for the third time since deciding to meet President Hinckley's challenge. This time, I found myself simply delighting both in the small details of language and in the overall messages that emerged. Pondering President Hinckley's promise, and reflecting on the joy I had recently felt in having his promise fulfilled in my own life, I decided that my approach to teaching the Book of Mormon would be to take my students on a quest to finish the book before the end of the year. This meant that we would be reading the entire Book of Mormon in the space of one quarter—and not even a full quarter at that, but more like eight weeks, because there had been a delay in the opening of our new institute building.

In trying to figure out the best way to get through the whole Book of Mormon in such a short time, I decided that I could not hope to organize the material by themes. Instead, it seemed apparent to me that the best approach would be simply to ask the students to read the entire book, something the Prophet had charged them to do anyway by the end of the year, and then use the time we had together to discuss highlights of our reading.

Working my way through the book in my third reading of the year, with an eye toward teaching the class, I found myself delighting in certain verses, so it was those verses that I chose to discuss in class. As we met each week and discussed these verses, along with some verses the students had found in their own reading, my delight grew, and my realization of the blessings that President Hinckley had promised grew steadily more vivid.

After going through the whole Book of Mormon in one brief quarter, having met President Hinckley's challenge, our institute class then went through the Book of Mormon more slowly over the rest of the school year, studying the first half during the Winter Quarter and the second half during the Spring Quarter. As I prepared for these "more leisurely" classes, I expanded my notes and began to think that I would like to get my thoughts down on paper. (Or, more accurately, I wanted to get them entered into my computer—the times have changed!) As I proceeded to enter more of my thoughts into the computer, I began to see that if I put my mind to it and kept my fingers busy at the keyboard, I could expand my notes into book form so that I could share my love of the Book of Mormon with others. Although it took longer than I ever dreamed it would, this book finally took shape after many early morning and late night sessions at the keyboard.

My intention in the pages that follow is not to present a doctrinal commentary on the Book of Mormon, although at times I will offer just that. Overall, though, what you will find in the pages that follow is not so much an objective commentary on the Book of Mormon as it is a subjective response to the Book of Mormon.

My method—which I hope you will find quite simple and straightforward—is simply to go through the Book of Mormon, quoting and discussing those verses and passages that caught my attention as I read the Book of Mormon that summer, in the hope that I can impart to you a sense of the sheer joy and delight to be found within the pages of this sacred volume of scripture.

If I am successful, perhaps you too will share in that joy that comes from reading and responding to the Book of Mormon. Ideally, you will find yourself—whether you did or did not finish your own reading of the Book of Mormon back in 2005—eager to read the Book of Mormon for yourself, whether this be your first reading, your dozenth, or your hundredth. I am confident that if you do so, you will find that President Hinckley's promise still applies.

Chapter 1

1 Nephi

> 1 Nephi 1:1 — I, Nephi, having been born of goodly parents, therefore I was taught somewhat in all the learning of my father; and having seen many afflictions in the course of my days, nevertheless, having been highly favored of the Lord in all my days; yea, having had a great knowledge of the goodness and the mysteries of God, therefore I make a record of my proceedings in my days.

Just about everyone who has ever read, attempted to read, or at least began, at one time or another, to look at the Book of Mormon can recite from memory at least the first eight words: "I, Nephi, having been born of goodly parents." But what does it mean to be "born of goodly parents"?

Did you notice the word *therefore* immediately following the phrase "born of goodly parents"? Nephi is offering a causal explanation of why he was taught somewhat in the learning of his father, not just paying tribute to the goodness of his parents. Although there have been testimonies given in many fast and testimony meetings about "goodly parents," as I have come to read the Book of Mormon more intently, I find myself agreeing with those scholars who have suggested that "goodly" here might well mean something more along the lines of "well off" than "righteous." Because Nephi's parents were well off, they were thus able to provide more time for his education than he might otherwise have been provided.

Of course, as we move forward in the Book of Mormon we also learn that Nephi is not the oldest brother, and we might wonder whether Laman and Lemuel were offered the same opportunities for learning that Nephi was afforded. Perhaps they were more interested in the business side of things, since we see later that they had considerable concern over the family fortune and Lehi's seeming willingness to cash it all in. Nephi apparently was more of a "humanities major," taking an interest in languages. You can certainly imagine how this difference in educational orientation and personality would lead to the fraternal clashes reported later in Nephi's account.

To think of *goodly* meaning "well off" rather than "righteous" does not mean to imply that Lehi and Sariah were not righteous. I would rather hear young people today bearing testimony of their parents' righteousness than of their parents' riches. In any event, thinking of Nephi's opening phrase in this different way has deepened my appreciation for his character.

As we move on through this first chapter of the Book of Mormon, we soon find that Nephi tells us of his intention in writing his record.

> 1 Nephi 1:20 — And when the Jews heard these things they were angry with him; yea, even as with the prophets of old, whom they had cast out, and stoned, and slain; and they also sought his life, that they might take it away. But behold, I, Nephi, will show unto you that the tender mercies of the Lord are over all those whom he hath chosen, because of their faith, to make them mighty even unto the power of deliverance.

The beautiful phrase "the tender mercies of the Lord" always captures my interest as I read this chapter, and this verse is one that often comes up in discussions about the Book of Mormon. As I read and reread this verse this time around, however, I found that this scripture throws an interesting light on the faith/works question.

According to this verse, the Lord extends His tender mercies "over all that He has chosen, because of their faith." The first thing this made me think about was the idea that we might be chosen because of our faith. Does this mean that some people are simply chosen to have salvation extended to them? Are all who have faith chosen? Is having faith the only way to be chosen? Would that mean that someone who is currently without faith could never be chosen?

So many questions! As my mind came up with these questions, my first thoughts were in the mode of the dialogues of Plato, wherein Socrates would ask questions along the lines, "Are certain things good because they are favored by the gods, or are they favored by the gods because they are good?"

Of course Nephi, educated as he might have been, was not trying to emulate Socrates. As a matter of fact, it was not Nephi asking these questions. Nephi was making a fairly straightforward declaration about the goodness of the Lord. It was I who was coming up with these distracting questions.

No, Nephi was not trying to make some sort of philosophical point about whom might be chosen and what "being chosen" might actually mean; instead, he was declaring that those who have faith and are thus chosen by the Lord are those "whom He hath chosen, because of their faith, to make them mighty even unto the power of deliverance."

This declaration gives a different perspective on the faith/works question. What we see from this scripture is how faith and works are integrated. Those who are chosen by the Lord because of their faith are then made mighty unto the power of deliverance, which can be read to mean that the Lord sustains them in their works by granting them the strength to follow the commandments. Therefore, we are not saved by our works or faith alone.

The Lord does not choose us for salvation arbitrarily. One of the things we will come to see in reading the Book of Mormon is that in order to be chosen by the Lord, we must choose the Lord and exercise faith in Him. To those who are chosen by the Lord because of their faith, He shows tender mercy by granting them the strength they will need to be disciples. We might paraphrase this by saying, "By grace we are saved after all we can do, and in all that we do we can be strengthened by grace" (see 2 Nephi 25:23).

> 1 Nephi 2:24 — And if it so be that they rebel against me, they shall be a scourge unto thy seed, to stir them up in the ways of remembrance.

Upon reading this verse, a question immediately comes to mind: "What is the deeper purpose of the scourge?" Those who have already read the Book of Mormon and are thus familiar with the ongoing conflict between the Nephites and Lamanites may tend to read this verse as nothing more than a straightforward prophecy of the future. If we stop there, however, we may be missing something that the Book of Mormon is trying to teach us.

First of all, note that the Lord indicates that by being a scourge to Nephi's seed, the descendants of his brothers will "stir them up in the ways of remembrance." If that remembrance takes the form of helping the descendants of Nephi to remember their covenants, then the scourge will, interestingly enough, have a positive effect.

By likening this scripture unto ourselves, perhaps we can be led to reflect on how the trials and problems we endure in our lives—our personal "scourges"—have not only a negative, but also a positive effect. They help us remember what is really important in our lives and, in so doing, turn our hearts to the Lord. Indeed, we might also reflect on and realize that the whole plan of salvation as taught in the scriptures and in the temple tell the story of how the Lord has allowed Satan to have some influence in our lives—to serve as a universal scourge. The benefit is we realize the paths of Satan lead not to joy but to heartache, and our hearts and minds can turn to the Lord when we realize what is really important in our lives.

> 1 Nephi 3:7 — And it came to pass that I, Nephi, said unto my father: I will go and do the things which the Lord hath commanded, for I know that the Lord giveth no commandments unto the children of men, save he shall prepare a way for them that they may accomplish the thing which he commandeth them.

Here is another famous passage from the Book of Mormon, one that is recited over and over again in class after class. Typically, the focus of these recitations is the principle of obedience, which is certainly an important principle to ponder. However, when I read these familiar words this time, I found myself not so much wondering at Nephi's great faith and subsequent obedience, but rather wondering how Nephi came to have such great faith at such a young age. Reflecting on this question, I realized that a previous passage offers a strong hint:

> 1 Nephi 2:16 — And it came to pass that I, Nephi, being exceedingly young, nevertheless being large in stature, and also having great desires to know of the mysteries of God, wherefore, I did cry unto the Lord; and behold he did visit me, and did soften my heart that I did believe all the words which had been spoken by my father; wherefore, I did not rebel against him like unto my brothers.

Nephi had sought to know the mysteries of God, even at a young age. The Lord had blessed him with faith, and from faith springs obedience. Indeed, in reflecting on these passages, we can quite readily see why Nephi had declared that the tender mercies of the Lord would strengthen those whom God had chosen because of their faith. Later in his account, Nephi explains more fully his stated intent in writing his story:

> 1 Nephi 6:4 — For the fulness of mine intent is that I may persuade men to come unto the God of Abraham, and the God of Isaac, and the God of Jacob, and be saved.
>
> 5 — Wherefore, the things which are pleasing unto the world I do not write, but the things which are pleasing unto God and unto those who are not of the world.

Nephi here reveals his fundamental mission, which is to bring souls to Christ, the same mission proclaimed today by our modern prophets. As Nephi's writings continue, as in his account of his father's vision in chapter 8, we see the centrality of Christ, and in chapter 10, he explicitly mentions the Holy Ghost, adding to our understanding of the Godhead. Then in chapter 11, Nephi is given this promise:

> 1 Nephi 11:6 — And when I had spoken these words, the Spirit cried with a loud voice, saying: Hosanna to the Lord, the most high God; for he is God over all the earth, yea, even above all. And blessed art thou, Nephi, because thou believest in the Son of the most high God; wherefore, thou shalt behold the things which thou hast desired.

This is a wonderful confirmation and promise: "because thou believest . . . thou shalt behold." Nephi, because of his great faith, experiences the vision of his father Lehi, but in amplified form.

> 1 Nephi 11:16 — And he said unto me: Knowest thou the condescension of God?
>
> 17 — And I said unto him: I know that he loveth his children; nevertheless, I do not know the meaning of all things.

As Nephi answers the angel's inquiry, he reveals something about himself. No, he may not know the meaning of all things, but he has a pure and abiding faith in the goodness of God. He may not know the meaning of the term *condescension,* but by knowing of God's love for His children, Nephi knows why God would condescend to come to earth and suffer among us. The wondrous vision revealed to him is quite miraculous, but surely this is another instance of faith preceding the miracle. Nephi did not believe because he saw; rather, he saw because he believed.

> 1 Nephi 14:18 — And it came to pass that the angel spake unto me, saying: Look!
>
> 19 — And I looked and beheld a man, and he was dressed in a white robe.
>
> 20 — And the angel said unto me: Behold one of the twelve apostles of the Lamb.
>
> 21 — Behold, he shall see and write the remainder of these things; yea, and also many things which have been.

22 — And he shall also write concerning the end of the world.

23 — Wherefore, the things which he shall write are just and true; and behold they are written in the book which thou beheld proceeding out of the mouth of the Jew; and at the time they proceeded out of the mouth of the Jew, or, at the time the book proceeded out of the mouth of the Jew, the things which were written were plain and pure, and most precious and easy to the understanding of all men.

24 — And behold, the things which this apostle of the Lamb shall write are many things which thou hast seen; and behold, the remainder shalt thou see.

25 — But the things which thou shalt see hereafter thou shalt not write; for the Lord God hath ordained the apostle of the Lamb of God that he should write them.

26 — And also others who have been, to them hath he shown all things, and they have written them; and they are sealed up to come forth in their purity, according to the truth which is in the Lamb, in the own due time of the Lord, unto the house of Israel.

27 — And I, Nephi, heard and bear record, that the name of the apostle of the Lamb was John, according to the word of the angel.

28 — And behold, I, Nephi, am forbidden that I should write the remainder of the things which I saw and heard; wherefore the things which I have written sufficeth me; and I have written but a small part of the things which I saw.

29 — And I bear record that I saw the things which my father saw, and the angel of the Lord did make them known unto me.

30 — And now I make an end of speaking concerning the things which I saw while I was carried away in the spirit; and if all the things which I saw are not written, the things which I have written are true. And thus it is. Amen.

Not only does Nephi experience the vision of his father, he is shown much more, some of which he writes but much of which he apparently does not. Note the mention of the Apostle John, which confirms the Beloved Apostle's status as a supreme visionary.

> 1 Nephi 15:8 — And I said unto them: Have ye inquired of the Lord?
> 9 — And they said unto me: We have not; for the Lord maketh no such thing known unto us.
> 10 — Behold, I said unto them: How is it that ye do not keep the commandments of the Lord? How is it that ye will perish, because of the hardness of your hearts?
> 11 — Do ye not remember the things which the Lord hath said?—If ye will not harden your hearts, and ask me in faith, believing that ye shall receive, with diligence in keeping my commandments, surely these things shall be made known unto you.

How many times have we heard the counseling question, "Have you prayed about it?" In reading the response that Nephi's brothers gave, we can sense the defiance in their attitude. This attitude seems to be what prompted Nephi to vent his frustration on them. Notice that he asks quite pointedly, "How is it that ye will perish?" rather than offering more timid counsel such as, "My brothers, if ye are not careful, ye could very well perish."

> 1 Nephi 15:18 — Wherefore, our father hath not spoken of our seed alone, but also of all the house of Israel, pointing to the covenant which should be fulfilled in the latter days; which covenant the Lord made to our father Abraham, saying: In thy seed shall all the kindreds of the earth be blessed.

The Abrahamic covenant is an endless source of fascination and comfort. Those who have studied Abraham, those who have been sealed in the temple, and those who have reflected on their heritage as a covenant people have all pondered and marveled at the promise made to the Patriarch. To hear Nephi testify of it early in his account is another confirmation of the power of that most wonderful covenant.

> 1 Nephi 16:1 — And now it came to pass that after I, Nephi, had made an end of speaking to my brethren, behold they said unto me: Thou hast declared unto us hard things, more than we are able to bear.
>
> 2 — And it came to pass that I said unto them that I knew that I had spoken hard things against the wicked, according to the truth; and the righteous have I justified, and testified that they should be lifted up at the last day; wherefore, the guilty taketh the truth to be hard, for it cutteth them to the very center.
>
> 3 — And now my brethren, if ye were righteous and were willing to hearken to the truth, and give heed unto it, that ye might walk uprightly before God, then ye would not murmur because of the truth, and say: Thou speakest hard things against us.

Something that struck me about this passage is how vividly the phrase "hard things" contrasts to Nephi's earlier phrase, "tender mercies." We are taught in the Book of Mormon about the necessity for opposition, and here are two concepts that clearly are opposites: hard things and tender mercies.

It can be a hard thing to recognize the tender mercies of the Lord. If our hearts are hard, only the most tender mercy will be strong enough to soften us—but when we do soften, how tender our hearts will be as we feel that mercy! We may even recognize the strength that comes through soft things such as forgiveness, patience, and love. We will recognize that the hard things we were taught about were offered with love and we will be thankful for the tender mercies proffered by our Lord.

Reading on in this chapter, we encounter physical objects that have an effect not only on Nephi, but on the whole group. First, there is Nephi's bow.

> 1 Nephi 16:18 — And it came to pass that as I, Nephi, went forth to slay food, behold, I did break my bow, which was made of fine steel; and after I did break my bow, behold, my brethren were angry with me because of the loss of my bow, for we did obtain no food.

Here, the failure of a physical thing leads to a spiritual crisis. When the bow breaks, even Nephi's visionary father begins to murmur. As a result, Nephi has to exert the "energy of his soul" to chasten his father and brothers. He also fashions a new bow and counsels with his father about where he should look for game, presumably more to reassure his father than to gain actual hunting advice. The counsel Nephi has given Lehi begins to sink in, and as the voice of the Lord comes to him, Lehi realizes what he has done and feels deep shame.

> 1 Nephi 16:25 — And it came to pass that the voice of the Lord came unto my father; and he was truly chastened because of his murmuring against the Lord, insomuch that he was brought down into the depths of sorrow.
>
> 26 — And it came to pass that the voice of the Lord said unto him: Look upon the ball, and behold the things which are written.
>
> 27 — And it came to pass that when my father beheld the things which were written upon the ball, he did fear and tremble exceedingly, and also my brethren and the sons of Ishmael and our wives.
>
> 28 — And it came to pass that I, Nephi, beheld the pointers which were in the ball, that they did work according to the faith and diligence and heed which we did give unto them.
>
> 29 — And there was also written upon them a new writing, which was plain to be read, which did give us understanding concerning the ways of the Lord; and it was written and changed from time to time, according to the faith and diligence which we gave unto it. And thus we see that by small means the Lord can bring about great things.

Following the account of the bow, we are given an account of the Liahona, another physical object with spiritual implications. In the account of the bow, we saw how the failure of a simple physical object could expose human weakness and doubt, triggering a spiritual crisis.

In the account of the Liahona, we are shown a small physical object that can provide spiritual direction if those seeking direction have adequate faith. In both cases, something small and physical is capable of revealing the spiritual state of those who possess it, or as Nephi summarizes it, "and thus we see that by small means the Lord can bring about great things."

> 1 Nephi 17:13 — And I will also be your light in the wilderness; and I will prepare the way before you, if it so be that ye shall keep my commandments; wherefore, inasmuch as ye shall keep my commandments ye shall be led towards the promised land; and ye shall know that it is by me that ye are led.
>
> 14 — Yea, and the Lord said also that: After ye have arrived in the promised land, ye shall know that I, the Lord, am God; and that I, the Lord, did deliver you from destruction; yea, that I did bring you out of the land of Jerusalem.
>
> 15 — Wherefore, I, Nephi, did strive to keep the commandments of the Lord, and I did exhort my brethren to faithfulness and diligence.

These verses spoken by the Lord to Nephi can be read as an allegory that describes our situation as followers of the Lord. He will be our light, preparing the way before us, guiding us as we obey His commandments, and leading us toward life eternal. What is most wonderful about living an obedient life, however, is we will know that it is indeed the Lord who is leading us. We are promised that comforting assurance, even as Nephi was promised with the knowledge that it was the Lord who had brought them out of destruction.

> 1 Nephi 19:23 — And I did read many things unto them which were written in the books of Moses; but that I might more fully persuade them to believe in the Lord their Redeemer I did read unto them that which was written by the prophet Isaiah; for I did liken all scriptures unto us, that it might be for our profit and learning.

In reading this verse we once again encounter the phrase, "liken the scriptures," a phrase that has been repeated in sacrament meeting talks, firesides, Sunday School lessons, and (I hope) family home evening lessons. Indeed, the injunction to "liken the scriptures unto us,"—which most of us, commendably, seem to remember as "liken the scriptures unto ourselves," or as the speakers and teachers are wont to phrase it, "liken the scriptures unto yourselves,"—is a principle we need to simultaneously put into and take out of our reading of the Book of Mormon.

When I taught my institute classes, I tried to make this one of my guiding principles and chief goals for each lesson—to beckon, persuade, or otherwise instigate the students to dig into the Book of Mormon and read what was written as though it were written expressly for them. At the same time, I tried to remember why Nephi had read to his people what was written in Isaiah. We learn that Nephi read and preached to his people the words of Isaiah that he might "more fully persuade them to believe in the Lord their Redeemer." So we must we also read the words of the Book of Mormon prophets in an effort to "more fully persuade [ourselves] to believe in the Lord [our] Redeemer." Moreover, we should let that be our end purpose as we read the scriptures and liken them unto ourselves: to come to Christ.

Indeed, when we make the effort to liken the scriptures unto ourselves, and as we gain from our reading and study of the Book of Mormon and other scriptures the insight that Christ is calling upon us to repent, come unto Him, and be saved, we will become more persuaded, and therefore more persuasive, when we seek to share our knowledge and joy with others.

> 1 Nephi 22:27 — And now behold, I, Nephi, say unto you that all these things must come according to the flesh.
>
> 28 — But, behold, all nations, kindreds, tongues, and people shall dwell safely in the Holy One of Israel if it so be that they will repent.
>
> 29 — And now I, Nephi, make an end; for I durst not speak further as yet concerning these things.
>
> 30 — Wherefore, my brethren, I would that ye should

> consider that the things which have been written upon the plates of brass are true; and they testify that a man must be obedient to the commandments of God.
>
> 31 — Wherefore, ye need not suppose that I and my father are the only ones that have testified, and also taught them. Wherefore, if ye shall be obedient to the commandments, and endure to the end, ye shall be saved at the last day. And thus it is. Amen.

Once again, Nephi speaks of what can be learned from the scriptures. Note that he first acknowledges that temptations and trials and destructions will come about because of the flesh, our mortal condition, before he goes on to speak of the ultimate triumph of the Lord. But Nephi assures us that through repenting and keeping the commandments, we can dwell safely in the Lord, and he reminds us that we have not only his word for it, but we also have the word of his father, Lehi, and of the scriptures.

What can we learn from this, beyond what is taught on the immediate surface? If we liken the scriptures unto ourselves, we might read Nephi as saying to us that although Lehi is gone, Nephi is gone, Joseph Smith is gone, and Gordon B. Hinckley is gone, all these prophets have taught us to repent and keep the commandments and endure to the end. Even after all these prophets are no longer with us, we will still have the scriptures (not only the four standard works but also our library of conference talks and other collected writings of our prophets) to teach us these saving doctrines.

Chapter 2

2 Nephi

Having mentioned his father, Lehi, as a witness of Christ at the close of 1 Nephi, Nephi then yields the pulpit to his father at the beginning of 2 Nephi. In the course of his sermon, Lehi reminds his hearers that:

> 2 Nephi 1:20 — And he hath said that: Inasmuch as ye shall keep my commandments ye shall prosper in the land; but inasmuch as ye will not keep my commandments ye shall be cut off from my presence.

This promise and warning are echoed throughout the Book of Mormon. As we continue our way through the Book of Mormon, we will surely see these words fulfilled in the history of the people. But as I read this verse and attempted to liken it unto myself, I began to see Lehi's statement not only as a warning about the promised land itself, but as a shadow or type of salvation. If we keep the commandments, we will prosper in our lives, at least in regard to the things of the Spirit, but if we do not keep the commandments, we will be cut off from that which we have been promised.

> 2 Nephi 1:23 — Awake, my sons; put on the armor of righteousness. Shake off the chains with which ye are bound, and come forth out of obscurity, and arise from the dust.

Along the lines of his injunction about keeping the commandments, Lehi offers this interesting language to make his point, although I do sometimes wonder why he did not start with taking off the chains, which would seem to be something we would do before we could then move on to putting on the "armor of righteousness." In any event, Lehi's language is striking, and his instruction is clear.

> 2 Nephi 2:1 — And now, Jacob, I speak unto you: Thou art my first-born in the days of my tribulation in the wilderness. And behold, in thy childhood thou hast suffered afflictions and much sorrow, because of the rudeness of thy brethren.
>
> 2 — Nevertheless, Jacob, my first-born in the wilderness, thou knowest the greatness of God; and he shall consecrate thine afflictions for thy gain

One of my favorite figures in the Book of Mormon has always been Jacob, that energetic, scholarly, brooding prophet, who is responsible for one of the most haunting verses in scripture: Jacob 7:26, which we will consider in due time. For now, note well the language of these first few verses of Lehi's blessing to Jacob, which is a fascinating foretaste of the language of that later verse.

As this blessing goes on, Lehi first talks about the importance of free agency and the mercy of the Messiah, and then he slips into the instructional mode that we will find over and over again in the Book of Mormon, the same instruction that we are counseled to use today: the "three pillars," which are the Creation, the Fall, and the Atonement. This is a powerful doctrinal chapter, worth reading and rereading.

> 2 Nephi 2:5 — And men are instructed sufficiently that they know good from evil. And the law is given unto men. And by the law no flesh is justified; or, by the law men are cut off. Yea, by the temporal law they were cut off; and also, by the spiritual law they perish from that which is good, and become miserable forever.
>
> 6 — Wherefore, redemption cometh in and through

the Holy Messiah; for he is full of grace and truth.

7 — Behold, he offereth himself a sacrifice for sin, to answer the ends of the law, unto all those who have a broken heart and a contrite spirit; and unto none else can the ends of the law be answered.

8 — Wherefore, how great the importance to make these things known unto the inhabitants of the earth, that they may know that there is no flesh that can dwell in the presence of God, save it be through the merits, and mercy, and grace of the Holy Messiah, who layeth down his life according to the flesh, and taketh it again by the power of the Spirit, that he may bring to pass the resurrection of the dead, being the first that should rise.

9 — Wherefore, he is the firstfruits unto God, inasmuch as he shall make intercession for all the children of men; and they that believe in him shall be saved.

10 — And because of the intercession for all, all men come unto God; wherefore, they stand in the presence of him, to be judged of him according to the truth and holiness which is in him. Wherefore, the ends of the law which the Holy One hath given, unto the inflicting of the punishment which is affixed, which punishment that is affixed is in opposition to that of the happiness which is affixed, to answer the ends of the atonement—

11 — For it must needs be, that there is an opposition in all things. If not so, my first-born in the wilderness, righteousness could not be brought to pass, neither wickedness, neither holiness nor misery, neither good nor bad. Wherefore, all things must needs be a compound in one; wherefore, if it should be one body it must needs remain as dead, having no life neither death, nor corruption nor incorruption, happiness nor misery, neither sense nor insensibility.

12 — Wherefore, it must needs have been created for a thing of naught; wherefore there would have been no purpose in the end of its creation. Wherefore, this thing must needs destroy the wisdom of God and his eternal

purposes, and also the power, and the mercy, and the justice of God.

13— And if ye shall say there is no law, ye shall also say there is no sin. If ye shall say there is no sin, ye shall also say there is no righteousness. And if there be no righteousness there be no happiness. And if there be no righteousness nor happiness there be no punishment nor misery. And if these things are not there is no God. And if there is no God we are not, neither the earth; for there could have been no creation of things, neither to act nor to be acted upon; wherefore, all things must have vanished away.

14 — And now, my sons, I speak unto you these things for your profit and learning; for there is a God, and he hath created all things, both the heavens and the earth, and all things that in them are, both things to act and things to be acted upon.

15 — And to bring about his eternal purposes in the end of man, after he had created our first parents, and the beasts of the field and the fowls of the air, and in fine, all things which are created, it must needs be that there was an opposition; even the forbidden fruit in opposition to the tree of life; the one being sweet and the other bitter.

16 — Wherefore, the Lord God gave unto man that he should act for himself. Wherefore, man could not act for himself save it should be that he was enticed by the one or the other.

17 — And I, Lehi, according to the things which I have read, must needs suppose that an angel of God, according to that which is written, had fallen from heaven; wherefore, he became a devil, having sought that which was evil before God.

18 — And because he had fallen from heaven, and had become miserable forever, he sought also the misery of all mankind. Wherefore, he said unto Eve, yea, even that old serpent, who is the devil, who is the father of all

lies, wherefore he said: Partake of the forbidden fruit, and ye shall not die, but ye shall be as God, knowing good and evil.

19 — And after Adam and Eve had partaken of the forbidden fruit they were driven out of the garden of Eden, to till the earth.

20 — And they have brought forth children; yea, even the family of all the earth.

21 — And the days of the children of men were prolonged, according to the will of God, that they might repent while in the flesh; wherefore, their state became a state of probation, and their time was lengthened, according to the commandments which the Lord God gave unto the children of men. For he gave commandment that all men must repent; for he showed unto all men that they were lost, because of the transgression of their parents.

22 — And now, behold, if Adam had not transgressed he would not have fallen, but he would have remained in the garden of Eden. And all things which were created must have remained in the same state in which they were after they were created; and they must have remained forever, and had no end.

23 — And they would have had no children; wherefore they would have remained in a state of innocence, having no joy, for they knew no misery; doing no good, for they knew no sin.

24 — But behold, all things have been done in the wisdom of him who knoweth all things.

25 — Adam fell that men might be; and men are, that they might have joy.

26 — And the Messiah cometh in the fulness of time, that he may redeem the children of men from the fall. And because that they are redeemed from the fall they have become free forever, knowing good from evil; to act for themselves and not to be acted upon, save it be by the punishment of the law at the great and last day, according to the commandments which God hath given.

> 27 — Wherefore, men are free according to the flesh; and all things are given them which are expedient unto man. And they are free to choose liberty and eternal life, through the great Mediator of all men, or to choose captivity and death, according to the captivity and power of the devil; for he seeketh that all men might be miserable like unto himself.
>
> 28 — And now, my sons, I would that ye should look to the great Mediator, and hearken unto his great commandments; and be faithful unto his words, and choose eternal life, according to the will of his Holy Spirit;
>
> 29 — And not choose eternal death, according to the will of the flesh and the evil which is therein, which giveth the spirit of the devil power to captivate, to bring you down to hell, that he may reign over you in his own kingdom.
>
> 30 — I have spoken these few words unto you all, my sons, in the last days of my probation; and I have chosen the good part, according to the words of the prophet. And I have none other object save it be the everlasting welfare of your souls. Amen.

So many times we open the Book of Mormon to 2 Nephi 2 just to read 2:25, that famous passage about joy, or maybe 2:11, that famous passage about the necessity for opposition in all things, but how much more rewarding it would be if we would take the extra time to read the whole chapter, which offers a penetrating analysis of the human condition. Not only does Lehi affirm the agency of man, but he puts agency into context, showing us both why we have it and what we must do with it. In so doing, he simultaneously encourages us to have joy while showing us where joy is to be found.

> 2 Nephi 4:15 — And upon these I write the things of my soul, and many of the scriptures which are engraven upon the plates of brass. For my soul delighteth in the scriptures, and my heart pondereth them, and writeth them for the learning and the profit of my children.

"My soul delighteth in the scriptures"—these are delightful words indeed, words that LDS parents long to hear from their children and that seminary and institute teachers long to hear from their students. Indeed, these are words we ourselves should long to hear in our own hearts.

> 2 Nephi 4:16 — Behold, my soul delighteth in the things of the Lord; and my heart pondereth continually upon the things which I have seen and heard.

"My soul delighteth in the things of the Lord"—these words fall so easily upon our ears and in our minds. We can hear the joy expressed by Nephi as he ponders his blessed state. In the following verses, we encounter the "Song of Nephi," which reminds us of the Psalms of David. As we read and ponder these verses, surely we will find our souls delighting in the scriptures. Surely we will find our hearts—not just our minds—pondering the things we have read, even if these things we have read cause us first to reflect upon our own sinful state, as did Nephi.

> 2 Nephi 4:17 — Nevertheless, notwithstanding the great goodness of the Lord, in showing me his great and marvelous works, my heart exclaimeth: O wretched man that I am! Yea, my heart sorroweth because of my flesh; my soul grieveth because of mine iniquities.
>
> 18 — I am encompassed about, because of the temptations and the sins which do so easily beset me.
>
> 19 — And when I desire to rejoice, my heart groaneth because of my sins; nevertheless, I know in whom I have trusted.
>
> 20 — My God hath been my support; he hath led me through mine afflictions in the wilderness; and he hath preserved me upon the waters of the great deep.
>
> 21 — He hath filled me with his love, even unto the consuming of my flesh.
>
> 22 — He hath confounded mine enemies, unto the causing of them to quake before me.

23 — Behold, he hath heard my cry by day, and he hath given me knowledge by visions in the night-time.

24 — And by day have I waxed bold in mighty prayer before him; yea, my voice have I sent up on high; and angels came down and ministered unto me.

25 — And upon the wings of his Spirit hath my body been carried away upon exceedingly high mountains. And mine eyes have beheld great things, yea, even too great for man; therefore I was bidden that I should not write them.

26 — O then, if I have seen so great things, if the Lord in his condescension unto the children of men hath visited men in so much mercy, why should my heart weep and my soul linger in the valley of sorrow, and my flesh waste away, and my strength slacken, because of mine afflictions?

27 — And why should I yield to sin, because of my flesh? Yea, why should I give way to temptations, that the evil one have place in my heart to destroy my peace and afflict my soul? Why am I angry because of mine enemy?

28 — Awake, my soul! No longer droop in sin. Rejoice, O my heart, and give place no more for the enemy of my soul.

29 — Do not anger again because of mine enemies. Do not slacken my strength because of mine afflictions.

30 — Rejoice, O my heart, and cry unto the Lord, and say: O Lord, I will praise thee forever; yea, my soul will rejoice in thee, my God, and the rock of my salvation.

31 — O Lord, wilt thou redeem my soul? Wilt thou deliver me out of the hands of mine enemies? Wilt thou make me that I may shake at the appearance of sin?

32 — May the gates of hell be shut continually before me, because that my heart is broken and my spirit is contrite! O Lord, wilt thou not shut the gates of thy righteousness before me, that I may walk in the path of the low valley, that I may be strict in the plain road!

33 — O Lord, wilt thou encircle me around in the

> robe of thy righteousness! O Lord, wilt thou make a way for mine escape before mine enemies! Wilt thou make my path straight before me! Wilt thou not place a stumbling block in my way—but that thou wouldst clear my way before me, and hedge not up my way, but the ways of mine enemy.
>
> 34 — O Lord, I have trusted in thee, and I will trust in thee forever. I will not put my trust in the arm of flesh; for I know that cursed is he that putteth his trust in the arm of flesh. Yea, cursed is he that putteth his trust in man or maketh flesh his arm.
>
> 35 — Yea, I know that God will give liberally to him that asketh. Yea, my God will give me, if I ask not amiss; therefore I will lift up my voice unto thee; yea, I will cry unto thee, my God, the rock of my righteousness. Behold, my voice shall forever ascend up unto thee, my rock and mine everlasting God. Amen.

Note above in verse 25 that Nephi writes of having visions so grand and powerful that he could not write them. Given the grand and powerful nature of those visions that he did write about, we can only ponder in curious wonder what else he might have seen.

> 2 Nephi 5:5 — And it came to pass that the Lord did warn me, that I, Nephi, should depart from them and flee into the wilderness, and all those who would go with me.

Suddenly it is time to depart, a common theme in the Book of Mormon. Can we think of times in our own lives when it was time to just get away? Have we ever been warned by the Spirit of people or situations that it would be best to leave behind? Have we knowingly or unknowingly visited websites that we suddenly realize we need to depart from and never return to again?

> 2 Nephi 6:2 — Behold, my beloved brethren, I, Jacob, having been called of God, and ordained after the manner of his holy order, and having been consecrated by my

> brother Nephi, unto whom ye look as a king or a protector, and on whom ye depend for safety, behold ye know that I have spoken unto you exceedingly many things.
>
> 3 — Nevertheless, I speak unto you again; for I am desirous for the welfare of your souls. Yea, mine anxiety is great for you; and ye yourselves know that it ever has been. For I have exhorted you with all diligence; and I have taught you the words of my father; and I have spoken unto you concerning all things which are written, from the creation of the world.
>
> 4 — And now, behold, I would speak unto you concerning things which are, and which are to come; wherefore, I will read you the words of Isaiah. And they are the words which my brother has desired that I should speak unto you. And I speak unto you for your sakes, that ye may learn and glorify the name of your God.

Jacob begins his address by establishing his authority. He says that he was called of God, ordained to the priesthood, and consecrated by his brother Nephi, whom, Jacob notes, the people have looked upon as a king or protector. He reminds them that he has spoken to them previously, and then goes on to say that he is deeply concerned about them.

In a pattern repeated over and over again in the Book of Mormon, Jacob then appeals to several witnesses, including the prophecies of his father and the teachings of scripture, starting with the Creation. He asserts that he is going to rely heavily upon the words of Isaiah (another prophetic pattern that we will encounter often as we read the Book of Mormon). He says that he will be teaching about things that are and things that are to come, inviting both his audience and us to "learn and glorify the name of God."

> 2 Nephi 6:8 — And now I, Jacob, would speak somewhat concerning these words. For behold, the Lord has shown me that those who were at Jerusalem, from whence we came, have been slain and carried away captive.
>
> 9 — Nevertheless, the Lord has shown unto me that they should return again. And he also has shown unto me

> that the Lord God, the Holy One of Israel, should manifest himself unto them in the flesh; and after he should manifest himself they should scourge him and crucify him, according to the words of the angel who spake it unto me.

We can sense that Jacob's great desire is to have his listeners both "liken the scriptures unto themselves" and hear his inspired testimony of Christ. See how Jacob makes it only two verses into Isaiah before he pauses to offer an interjection in which he reminds those assembled of their history and their future, in both of which Jacob sees the role of the Savior. For many of us who read the Book of Mormon today, the Isaiah passages are something to be endured rather than savored. If only we had the enthusiasm and vision of Jacob! He loves these scriptures and he believes deeply that pondering them will help us to understand our situation and our future. He also believes that as we ponder the scriptures, especially the prophecies of Isaiah, we will come to have a greater understanding of Christ.

> 2 Nephi 7:4 — The Lord God hath given me the tongue of the learned, that I should know how to speak a word in season unto thee, O house of Israel. When ye are weary he waketh morning by morning. He waketh mine ear to hear as the learned.

I have no idea of how many times in my life I must have read this verse as I made my way through the Book of Mormon, but until my second time through in responding to President Hinckley's challenge, I had never noticed the interesting sentence that suddenly grabbed my attention, "When ye are weary He waketh morning by morning." What a concise and clever characterization of the Lord! Every day we face trials that take something out of us. We get tired—physically weary, mentally depleted, emotionally drained—to the point where we can get downright discouraged. There may be mornings when we have to struggle to get out of bed and face the day. But the Lord is always there; each day is a new day, and we can take comfort and hope, knowing that He is there to hear and answer our prayers.

> 2 Nephi 9:3 — Behold, my beloved brethren, I speak unto you these things that ye may rejoice, and lift up your heads forever, because of the blessings which the Lord God shall bestow upon your children.

In the opening verse of this chapter, Jacob tells his listeners that he has read to them the words of Isaiah so that they would know of the covenants the Lord has made with the house of Israel. In this verse, he reminds both his listeners and us once again of the joy and hope that studying the scriptures can bring. When we ponder the covenants made to our ancestors, we can rejoice in the blessings that are in store for our children. This same joy can come to us as we ponder the blessing of the temple, for in the temple we secure and contemplate the covenants the Lord established with our ancestors, even as we look forward to the blessings that being sealed to our eternal families will bring our children and their children to come.

> 2 Nephi 9:6 — For as death hath passed upon all men, to fulfil the merciful plan of the great Creator, there must needs be a power of resurrection, and the resurrection must needs come unto man by reason of the fall; and the fall came by reason of transgression; and because man became fallen they were cut off from the presence of the Lord.
>
> 7 — Wherefore, it must needs be an infinite atonement—save it should be an infinite atonement this corruption could not put on incorruption. Wherefore, the first judgment which came upon man must needs have remained to an endless duration. And if so, this flesh must have laid down to rot and to crumble to its mother earth, to rise no more.

Here we have another wonderful chapter that is simply bursting with expressive language. You can sense the sheer power of Jacob's testimony as he begins by extolling the infinite Atonement, which saves us from the fate that we have all seen evidence of—flesh eventually rotting and crumbling into the earth, seemingly gone forever along with all hopes, dreams, and aspirations. But Jacob does not fall into despair, nor need we despair as we read these following verses and contemplate and celebrate the attributes of our God.

> 2 Nephi 9:8 — O the wisdom of God, his mercy and grace! For behold, if the flesh should rise no more our spirits must become subject to that angel who fell from before the presence of the Eternal God, and became the devil, to rise no more.

Wisdom, mercy, and grace—do we sense how deeply these attributes seem to be bound together? We see them in our God and, as we seek them in our own hearts, we realize that the pursuit of wisdom brings us grace and mercy.

> 2 Nephi 9:10 — O how great the goodness of our God, who prepareth a way for our escape from the grasp of this awful monster; yea, that monster, death and hell, which I call the death of the body, and also the death of the spirit.

As we come to behold the wisdom, grace, and mercy of God, we bow humbled before His goodness. Reading these words, we can sense in our own hearts how wisdom, grace, and mercy are essential things that we need in our lives to escape the death of our spirits. We come to realize that we will never seize goodness by force or cunning, but only through wise and humbly obedient means; even then, it will only be through the grace and mercy of God that we can hope to achieve real goodness. At that point, we may well cry out as did Jacob:

> 2 Nephi 9:13 — O how great the plan of our God! For on the other hand, the paradise of God must deliver up the spirits of the righteous, and the grave deliver up the body of the righteous; and the spirit and the body is restored to itself again, and all men become incorruptible, and immortal, and they are living souls, having a perfect knowledge like unto us in the flesh, save it be that our knowledge shall be perfect.

"O how great the plan of our God!" Even though our lives are part of that plan, we are humbled by it even as we rejoice in its very existence, even as we rejoice in our knowledge of the existence of our God. The Book of Mormon helps us to look at life as something that is part of a plan. Believing that life is part of a plan gives us a sense that our lives have purpose. Believing that our lives have a purpose gives us good reason to look forward to the future; thus we avoid depression and despair, which often stem from the lack of a perceived future. Although we know that our lives may not be trouble-free, our knowledge that life is part of God's plan gives us great hope and joy.

> 2 Nephi 9:14 — Wherefore, we shall have a perfect knowledge of all our guilt, and our uncleanness, and our nakedness; and the righteous shall have a perfect knowledge of their enjoyment, and their righteousness, being clothed with purity, yea, even with the robe of righteousness.

Do we want to be part of the "we" that shall have a perfect knowledge of all our guilt, or do we want to be part of the righteous that will have a perfect knowledge of their enjoyment? This may be the ultimate good news/bad news scenario:

- **The Good News:** You will someday come to have perfect knowledge.
- **The Bad News:** What you will know perfectly is your guilt and uncleanness.

That is not the way it has to be, of course. If the Book of Mormon teaches nothing else, it teaches us about the great plan of God, which is that through the atonement of Jesus Christ, we can choose to repent and have our sins forgiven, which leads to a much more hopeful bad news/good new scenario:

- **The Bad News:** You have done things in your life that have made you guilty and unclean.
- **The Good News:** If you will humble yourself and repent, you can be forgiven and cleansed through the atoning sacrifice of Jesus Christ.

> 2 Nephi 9:17 — O the greatness and the justice of our God! For he executeth all his words, and they have gone forth out of his mouth, and his law must be fulfilled.

Through justice we know that there are consequences to our actions. Acts of sin separate us from God, but acts of repentance can enable us to be brought back safely under His wing.

> 2 Nephi 9:19 — O the greatness of the mercy of our God, the Holy One of Israel! For he delivereth his saints from that awful monster the devil, and death, and hell, and that lake of fire and brimstone, which is endless torment.

That promised opportunity to be able to rise above our sins makes us realize how wonderful indeed is the mercy of the Lord. How wonderful indeed are those tender mercies that He extends to those who choose to come unto him!

> 2 Nephi 9:20 — O how great the holiness of our God! For he knoweth all things, and there is not anything save he knows it.

As we think of the great plan of salvation and how wonderful it is that the Lord has extended His mercy to us, we too can feel that sense of "how great the holiness of our God." The temples have written upon them the words, "Holiness to the Lord." So too should those words be written upon our hearts.

Jacob then moves on to express some "wo's" in verses 27 and beyond. As we read these warnings, let us pay special attention to verse 29.

> 2 Nephi 9:27 — But wo unto him that has the law given, yea, that has all the commandments of God, like unto us, and that transgresseth them, and that wasteth the days of his probation, for awful is his state!
>
> 28 — O that cunning plan of the evil one! O the vainness, and the frailties, and the foolishness of men! When they are learned they think they are wise, and they hearken not unto the counsel of God, for they set it aside, supposing they know of themselves, wherefore,

their wisdom is foolishness and it profiteth them not. And they shall perish.

29 — But to be learned is good if they hearken unto the counsels of God.

30 — But wo unto the rich, who are rich as to the things of the world. For because they are rich they despise the poor, and they persecute the meek, and their hearts are upon their treasures; wherefore, their treasure is their god. And behold, their treasure shall perish with them also.

31 — And wo unto the deaf that will not hear; for they shall perish.

32 — Wo unto the blind that will not see; for they shall perish also.

33 — Wo unto the uncircumcised of heart, for a knowledge of their iniquities shall smite them at the last day.

34 — Wo unto the liar, for he shall be thrust down to hell.

35 — Wo unto the murderer who deliberately killeth, for he shall die.

36 — Wo unto them who commit whoredoms, for they shall be thrust down to hell.

37 — Yea, wo unto those that worship idols, for the devil of all devils delighteth in them.

38 — And, in fine, wo unto all those who die in their sins; for they shall return to God, and behold his face, and remain in their sins.

Verse 29 reminds us of the promise of knowledge. Although temptations are many and pitfalls abundant, the path of knowledge can lead us to happiness if we learn not only the things of the world but also the ways of the Lord. The Greek philosophers counseled us to know ourselves. There is certainly wisdom in that injunction, for by knowing ourselves we will be able to make allowances for our weaknesses and accentuate our strengths.

However, we must always keep in mind the teaching of the Lord in John 17:3 that "this is life eternal, that they might know thee the only true God, and Jesus Christ, whom thou hast sent." Let us not be as the deaf that will not hear, or the blind who will not see.

> 2 Nephi 9:41 — O then, my beloved brethren, come unto the Lord, the Holy One. Remember that his paths are righteous. Behold, the way for man is narrow, but it lieth in a straight course before him, and the keeper of the gate is the Holy One of Israel; and he employeth no servant there; and there is none other way save it be by the gate; for he cannot be deceived, for the Lord God is his name.

To my mind, this is one of the most beautiful and most inspirational verses in all of scripture. The way before us is narrow, but it is laid out in a straight path before us. On the one hand, it can seem daunting to think that the way before us is narrow, but on the other hand, the narrowness of the path can be an advantage in helping us to focus on it. When we lose the way, many other paths may beckon to us, and our journey may seem to be more and more complicated.

But if we can stay on that narrow path, we are promised that the keeper of the gate is the Lord himself, and it is before Him that we will one day stand to see whether we are worthy of further passage through the gate. As we journey along in this life, let us always keep that promise in mind. He will be there to welcome us.

I can vividly recall the day I went through the Salt Lake Temple when the late Elder Carlos Asay was the temple president. As our group prepared to enter the first instruction room, there stood President Asay at the doorway, dressed in his white suit, greeting each member with a firm handshake and a warm smile. It was a wonderful feeling to be welcomed at the doorway to the temple by someone whom I recognized from seeing him speak in General Conference. Can you imagine how it will feel to be welcomed by the Savior himself at the gateway to the next life?

> 2 Nephi 9:50 — Come, my brethren, every one that thirsteth, come ye to the waters; and he that hath no money, come buy and eat; yea, come buy wine and milk without money and without price.

> 51 — Wherefore, do not spend money for that which is of no worth, nor your labor for that which cannot satisfy. Hearken diligently unto me, and remember the words which I have spoken; and come unto the Holy One of Israel, and feast upon that which perisheth not, neither can be corrupted, and let your soul delight in fatness.

This is such a joyous invitation! I often regret to see how for those who have become estranged from the Church, the scriptures are often recalled as a compendium of strict commandments and dire warnings that are perceived in a joyless, even fearful, way. One of the central messages of the Book of Mormon, however, is the happiness and joy that the gospel can bring. If only we can bring this message and extend this invitation to those we know and love who have left the path!

> 2 Nephi 10:23 — Therefore, cheer up your hearts, and remember that ye are free to act for yourselves—to choose the way of everlasting death or the way of eternal life.

Cheer up! You are free to choose! Again, this is such a joyful message. It is not always easy to choose that which is right, but at all times we are free to do so. Each day brings new opportunities. The Book of Mormon makes this startlingly clear.

> 2 Nephi 11:2 — And now I, Nephi, write more of the words of Isaiah, for my soul delighteth in his words. For I will liken his words unto my people, and I will send them forth unto all my children, for he verily saw my Redeemer, even as I have seen him.
>
> 3 — And my brother, Jacob, also has seen him as I have seen him; wherefore, I will send their words forth unto my children to prove unto them that my words are true. Wherefore, by the words of three, God hath said, I will establish my word. Nevertheless, God sendeth more witnesses, and he proveth all his words.
>
> 4 — Behold, my soul delighteth in proving unto my people the truth of the coming of Christ; for, for this end

> hath the law of Moses been given; and all things which have been given of God from the beginning of the world, unto man, are the typifying of him.
>
> 5 — And also my soul delighteth in the covenants of the Lord which he hath made to our fathers; yea, my soul delighteth in his grace, and in his justice, and power, and mercy in the great and eternal plan of deliverance from death.

Nephi, like his brother Jacob, loves the words of Isaiah. Furthermore, just as Isaiah has seen the Lord, so has Nephi, and so has his brother Jacob. Nephi delights in this knowledge, and we can take delight from reading his testimony. We can also delight as he does in the covenants the Lord made with our fathers: those covenants we read about in the scriptures, those covenants we renew in the temple.

As Jacob so testified, Nephi now testifies of the sheer joy he finds in considering the grace, justice, power, mercy, and great plan of the Lord. Nephi has pondered the words of Isaiah, he has pondered the words of his brother Jacob, and now he is adding his own witness. We would do well to ponder Nephi's witness, and having pondered, to add our own witness for others to hear and ponder.

> 2 Nephi 15:20 — Wo unto them that call evil good, and good evil, that put darkness for light, and light for darkness, that put bitter for sweet, and sweet for bitter!

This is an old warning, one that prophets have doubtless been issuing since time immemorial, but each time we read it, it seems fresh and relevant. In our time, we see examples all around us of calling evil good and good evil. All we have to do is to read the paper, watch the television, or surf the World Wide Web.

> 2 Nephi 25:1 — Now I, Nephi, do speak somewhat concerning the words which I have written, which have been spoken by the mouth of Isaiah. For behold, Isaiah spake many things which were hard for many of my

> people to understand; for they know not concerning the manner of prophesying among the Jews.

Nephi loves the words of Isaiah, but he knows that Isaiah is difficult to understand. Nephi's brethren had a hard time fully understanding these words, and so do we. This is another bonus of the Book of Mormon, that from time to time we are able to receive plainspoken explanation and counsel from prophets, such as Nephi, who have digested Isaiah's message.

> 2 Nephi 25:19 — For according to the words of the prophets, the Messiah cometh in six hundred years from the time that my father left Jerusalem; and according to the words of the prophets, and also the word of the angel of God, his name shall be Jesus Christ, the Son of God.
>
> 20 — And now, my brethren, I have spoken plainly that ye cannot err. And as the Lord God liveth that brought Israel up out of the land of Egypt, and gave unto Moses power that he should heal the nations after they had been bitten by the poisonous serpents, if they would cast their eyes unto the serpent which he did raise up before them, and also gave him power that he should smite the rock and the water should come forth; yea, behold I say unto you, that as these things are true, and as the Lord God liveth, there is none other name given under heaven save it be this Jesus Christ, of which I have spoken, whereby man can be saved.

Having previously stated his intention to speak plainly concerning the words of Isaiah, Nephi now speaks quite plainly of his own knowledge of the Redeemer. His words here are a notable example of "bearing down in pure testimony," a concept to which we will return later. For now, just bask in the power of his words and contemplate how your own strong and direct words of testimony might influence those who hear them. Those whom you teach, those whom you love the most—your family, your students, your home or visiting teaching families, your ward members—all can benefit greatly from hearing your strong and sincere testimony, directly and plainly spoken.

> 2 Nephi 25:23 — For we labor diligently to write, to persuade our children, and also our brethren, to believe in Christ, and to be reconciled to God; for we know that it is by grace that we are saved, after all we can do.

When I had read this verse on previous occasions, I would typically focus my attention on the phrase following the semicolon: "for we know that it is by grace we are saved, after all we can do." This time around, however, I found myself contemplating that first phrase, "We labor diligently." It suddenly struck me that sometimes, our church and family responsibilities really do involve work. Our church leaders really do labor diligently. Being a bishop or a stake president or a primary teacher—or a parent—really does require that we labor diligently to persuade those under our stewardship to believe and to be reconciled.

As I thought about this verse in that light, it also struck me that perhaps my previous understanding of the phrase beyond the semicolon had also been incomplete. I had tended to think of the phrase "all we can do" as equivalent to keeping the commandments. My problem in this was that I was thinking of "keeping the commandments" in a narrowly legalistic sense, not appreciating the actual labor and commitment that we need to put into our efforts. Keeping the commandments is more than simply choosing the right; it is laboring diligently in doing the right.

As I thought more about this verse, I also began to see more clearly why we so often encounter the terms "obedience" and "sacrifice" paired together. We must not merely obey, we must sacrifice. Indeed, there are many instances in which to obey requires that we sacrifice.

We must not only do what is right, we must work at doing what is right; indeed, we must labor diligently, until we have done all that we can do. Even then, we still need the grace of the Lord to ensure our salvation.

> 2 Nephi 25:26 — And we talk of Christ, we rejoice in

> Christ, we preach of Christ, we prophesy of Christ, and we write according to our prophecies, that our children may know to what source they may look for a remission of their sins.
>
> 27 — Wherefore, we speak concerning the law that our children may know the deadness of the law; and they, by knowing the deadness of the law, may look forward unto that life which is in Christ, and know for what end the law was given. And after the law is fulfilled in Christ, that they need not harden their hearts against him when the law ought to be done away.

I have often heard the first few phrases of verse 26 discussed as missionary-oriented evidence that the Book of Mormon does indeed testify of Christ and that Mormons are indeed Christians. Occasionally, I have heard the final phrase discussed as an example of the kinds of things we ought to be doing in our primary and youth classes and in our family home evenings—teaching our children about the source of the remission of sins. This is a noble aim, and we find this verse easy and natural to liken unto ourselves.

How many times, though, have we just skipped right over the next verse? Have we ever encountered a Primary or Sunday School lesson wherein the stated aim was to teach our children about the deadness of the law?

In my experience, I have seen that when people say that they are teaching our children about the law, their true intention is often quite the opposite—they are actually trying to "lay down the law," teaching principles such as "the commandments may appear to restrict your freedom, but by following them, you will become more free in the long run."

Although such principles may be true and valuable, such teaching hardly seems to be an example of teaching "the deadness of the law." If anything, teachings as these seem to be affirming not the deadness, but rather the vitality of the law.

It could be argued that Nephi is not speaking about what today we broadly refer to as "the commandments," but is rather speaking more specifically about what we today call "the Mosaic law." We have indeed taught our Sunday School students in our day about the deadness of that law. The problem is that to our youth today, the Mosaic law is something ancient and dead, and they do not really need to be convinced of its deadness.

This may be true, but to those who first listened to Nephi or Paul teach about the deadness of the law, they were hearing about a law that was part of the living fabric of their lives. The Mosaic Law was very much alive.

In our day, then, I would argue that as much as it may be important to remind our youth of the importance of keeping the commandments, it is equally important to teach them that it is by grace they are saved, after all they can do—that although it is important to keep the commandments, they will not save themselves by doing so. It is in that sense that we must teach them of the deadness of the law: not in the sense of the dead Mosaic Law, but rather in the sense that they must come to realize the commandments do not give life in and of themselves. Without the mercy and Atonement of the Savior, and without His gospel of repentance, merely obeying the commandments will not save any of us from spiritual death.

> 2 Nephi 26:1 —And after Christ shall have arisen from the dead he shall show himself unto you, my children, and my beloved brethren; and the words which he shall speak unto you shall be the law which ye shall do.

After his discussion about the necessity of teaching our children the deadness of the law, Nephi then offers his prophetic insight into higher things. The words of Christ shall be the law. Today, this is what we must strive to teach our children. The words of Christ must become their law. The words of Christ are what they must have written in their hearts.

Just a paragraph ago, I wrote that we must be careful to teach our children that mere obedience to the law will not save them, but now I am saying that we must strive to teach our children that the words of Christ shall be their law. Am I contradicting myself? I hope not.

We must of course teach our children to obey the commandments of God. Furthermore, we must teach them that Christ is the author of the law, and that there is no other name under heaven by which they can be saved. But we must not teach them that they will be saved by mere obedience to the law and the commandments. It is inevitable that they will not keep all the commandments, and unless they are taught that they can still be saved through repentance, through turning to their Savior, the most fundamental teaching of the gospel, they will not truly "get it."

Indeed, in my own personal experience of grappling with my sins, and in my experience as bishop in helping others to do the same, I have found that one of the most difficult concepts for many Saints to grasp is that they can be forgiven, that Christ truly is merciful. I have found that in our emphasis on keeping the commandments—and I am in no way denying or belittling the importance of keeping the commandments—we can forget about the power of repentance. We realize that we have sinned, and we see that no matter how many commandments we do keep, we have not been able to keep all of the commandments all of the time. In truth, we may come to feel that we can never hope to keep them all. If we are not mindful of the power of repentance, and the mercy of the Lord, we will find ourselves in the unenviable position of discovering for ourselves the deadness of the law while at the same time concluding that the deadness of the law means that we ourselves are dead—and without hope. What a sad state of affairs!

Recall that Joseph Smith was enjoined by the Lord to "say nothing but repentance unto this generation" (D&C 6:9). We sometimes think that means that he was supposed to continually call on the wicked to repent, but as we read the Book of Mormon, we can come to see that repentance is not just for the wicked, it is for all of us. Repentance is not just about justice, it is even more so about mercy. We need to not only call people to repentance, but also preach to them about repentance, which means that we need to teach and testify of the grace, mercy, and atoning sacrifice of the Lord.

We must come to realize that the Lord has instructed His prophets, ancient and modern, to call upon His people to repent, but that He has done so out of love, in the hope that we will return to Him and be made whole. As Nephi declares:

> 2 Nephi 26:25 — Behold, doth he cry unto any, saying: Depart from me? Behold, I say unto you, Nay; but he saith: Come unto me all ye ends of the earth, buy milk and honey, without money and without price.

Does the Lord ask any to depart? No. Will all be saved? No, not all will be saved; only those who repent and come unto Christ—only those who accept His loving invitation. Again, the charge we have been given to call people to repentance is not a charge intended to drive people away; it is instead a charge for us to invite the world to come unto Christ.

> 2 Nephi 26:30 — Behold, the Lord hath forbidden this thing; wherefore, the Lord God hath given a commandment that all men should have charity, which charity is love. And except they should have charity they were nothing. Wherefore, if they should have charity they would not suffer the laborer in Zion to perish.
>
> 31 — But the laborer in Zion shall labor for Zion; for if they labor for money they shall perish.

In my previous readings of the Book of Mormon, it had never occurred to me that the word *charity* was used so early in the text. I remembered that charity was discussed in Alma, in language similar to that used by Paul in Corinthians, but I had somehow glossed over this reference in the early pages of the Book of Mormon.

Not only was I surprised during this reading to see that Nephi had discussed charity, but I was also surprised to see that in the very first mention of charity in the Book of Mormon, it is given as a commandment. We are commanded to have charity.

At first, this seemed a bit strange to me. *Nephi is saying that we are commanded to have charity? Can this really be true?*

At some point it suddenly hit me: what did the Savior himself point to as the two commandments upon which hang all the law and the prophets? Number one was a commandment to love, and number two was a commandment to love. Although I had certainly been a mite slow on the uptake, I was suddenly able to see the utter obviousness of what Nephi was saying. Why had it seemed strange to think of charity as being a commandment? Why had I never noticed or thought about this before?

Although I now recognized the first two commandments had to do with love, something about commanding us to have charity still bothered me. As I reflected further on this, I came to see that when I considered the commandments to love God and to love my neighbor, I looked at these as commandments about what I should do. If I attended church, performed my priesthood duties, said my prayers, avoided profane language, and bore my testimony, I was showing my love for God. (Now, there was that little technicality about loving God with *all* my heart, might, mind and soul, but I tended to gloss over that—at least in doing the sorts of things I just mentioned, I could say that I was trying mightily to love God.)

Likewise, if I was kind to strangers, helpful to widows, and a trustworthy friend, I was on my way toward loving my neighbor as myself. By doing these sorts of things, I could at least say that I was giving it an honest try, after all.

But when I read the language that Nephi used, saying that I had been commanded to have charity, not just to do charitable things, I realized that the Lord did not want me to merely go through the motions, acting as though I had love in my heart—he was actually commanding me to have love in my heart, to be charitable. I would then do charitable things naturally because of my charitable, more Christlike nature.

As I began to reflect upon these verses, I came to realize more vividly than ever before that I will not be judged for what I do, but for what I am. The commandment to have charity seemed at first to be an overwhelming commandment, but the more I thought about it, the more I realized that this was what the Atonement was all about: to give us the chance to transcend our limitations through the intervening ministrations of the Spirit, and to be truly illuminated by the light of Christ.

Finally, then, peace came upon me. I came to understand what I should have understood all along: the good news of the Gospel, the deeper meaning of repentance as a turning from sin to God, not just in our outward actions, but deep within our hearts.

I then remembered something President Hinckley had promised when he issued his challenge: no matter how many times we had read the Book of Mormon before, there would come into our lives an added measure of the Spirit if we would read it again. At least for some of us, to be able grasp the obvious, we truly need that extra measure of the Spirit.

If we have charity, we will not allow the laborer in Zion to perish. We will practice kindness and compassion. We will love our neighbors as ourselves. As we do so, we ourselves become laborers in Zion. We labor not for money but for Zion. In other words, as we labor for the pure in heart, we become pure in heart, not as a direct result of our labors, but as a result of the grace of the Lord after all we can do.

> 2 Nephi 26:33 — For none of these iniquities come of the Lord; for he doeth that which is good among the children of men; and he doeth nothing save it be plain unto the children of men; and he inviteth them all to come unto him and partake of his goodness; and he denieth none that come unto him, black and white, bond and free, male and female; and he remembereth the heathen; and all are alike unto God, both Jew and Gentile.

This is one of those beautiful verses in the Book of Mormon over which I feel compelled to linger each time I read it. All are invited to come unto Christ, all are invited to partake of His goodness, and all are declared to be alike before God. The mission of the Church is to invite all to come unto Christ, both the living and the dead, and thus we have our great missionary effort, our great temple effort, our great building program, our great worldwide media, and other vehicles for inviting and delivering souls to the Master.

> 2 Nephi 31:2 — Wherefore, the things which I have written sufficeth me, save it be a few words which I must speak concerning the doctrine of Christ; wherefore, I shall

speak unto you plainly, according to the plainness of my prophesying.

3 — For my soul delighteth in plainness; for after this manner doth the Lord God work among the children of men. For the Lord God giveth light unto the understanding; for he speaketh unto men according to their language, unto their understanding.

When I read that Nephi's soul "delighteth in plainness," I want to say that my soul delighteth in the Book of Mormon, which makes plain the Atonement, the plan of happiness, and the gospel and doctrine of Christ. I can imagine later keepers of the plates reading these words of Nephi, contemplating them, and vowing to keep the record plain as they recorded their own and others' thoughts and prophecies concerning the doctrines of Christ.

2 Nephi 31:16 — And now, my beloved brethren, I know by this that unless a man shall endure to the end, in following the example of the Son of the living God, he cannot be saved.

17 — Wherefore, do the things which I have told you I have seen that your Lord and your Redeemer should do; for, for this cause have they been shown unto me, that ye might know the gate by which ye should enter. For the gate by which ye should enter is repentance and baptism by water; and then cometh a remission of your sins by fire and by the Holy Ghost.

18 — And then are ye in this strait and narrow path which leads to eternal life; yea, ye have entered in by the gate; ye have done according to the commandments of the Father and the Son; and ye have received the Holy Ghost, which witnesses of the Father and the Son, unto the fulfilling of the promise which he hath made, that if ye entered in by the way ye should receive.

19 — And now, my beloved brethren, after ye have gotten into this strait and narrow path, I would ask if all is done? Behold, I say unto you, Nay; for ye have not come thus far save it were by the word of Christ with unshaken

> faith in him, relying wholly upon the merits of him who is mighty to save.
>
> 20 — Wherefore, ye must press forward with a steadfastness in Christ, having a perfect brightness of hope, and a love of God and of all men. Wherefore, if ye shall press forward, feasting upon the word of Christ, and endure to the end, behold, thus saith the Father: Ye shall have eternal life.
>
> 21 — And now, behold, my beloved brethren, this is the way; and there is none other way nor name given under heaven whereby man can be saved in the kingdom of God. And now, behold, this is the doctrine of Christ, and the only and true doctrine of the Father, and of the Son, and of the Holy Ghost, which is one God, without end. Amen.

We must endure to the end if we are to be saved. That might seem daunting to some, but the passages that follow offer encouragement and hope. We can repent, be baptized, strive to follow the commandments, and live a repentant, faithful life. As Nephi says, we must press forward. He does not tell us to run forward, nor to leap forward; he tells us to press forward. We will experience opposition. We will experience discouragement, particularly and most discouragingly our own weaknesses and shortcomings. But if we press forward, holding to the rod, feasting upon the word, our hope and our effort will not be in vain. To grasp that possibility is indeed to obtain a perfect brightness of hope.

> 2 Nephi 32:3 — Angels speak by the power of the Holy Ghost; wherefore, they speak the words of Christ. Wherefore, I said unto you, feast upon the words of Christ; for behold, the words of Christ will tell you all things what ye should do.

Once again we are invited to feast—feast!—upon the words of Christ. We are told that angels speak the words of Christ. As I read this passage, I find myself thinking of the angel Moroni, who taught Joseph Smith and who brought us the Book of Mormon. I also think of Gordon B. Hinckley, who issued this challenge to feast upon the words of Christ as found in the Book of Mormon. Let us follow Nephi, Moroni, Joseph Smith, and Gordon B. Hinckley—let us feast indeed!

> 2 Nephi 33:6 — I glory in plainness; I glory in truth; I glory in my Jesus for he hath redeemed my soul from hell.

Here we see the faith of Nephi in powerful plainness. His straightforward affirmation bears powerful testimony of his faith in and love for the Savior.

The Savior taught that we need to become as little children. Nephi's affirmation has a childlike simplicity and directness that shows he has the humble faith that the Savior desired of those who would truly be His disciples.

Chapter 3

Jacob

To me, Jacob is one of the most fascinating figures in the Book of Mormon, and I am always excited about getting to Jacob when I read the Book of Mormon. In my mind, I always picture a serious young man studying the scriptures and absorbing the teachings of his father and his brother, a serious young man who gives much thought to what he is taught. From his teachings, we can see that he has pondered the human condition and has come to apply gospel principles to the conduct of human life.

> Jacob 2:17 — Think of your brethren like unto yourselves, and be familiar with all and free with your substance, that they may be rich like unto you.
>
> 18 — But before ye seek for riches, seek ye for the kingdom of God.
>
> 19 — And after ye have obtained a hope in Christ ye shall obtain riches, if ye seek them; and ye will seek them for the intent to do good—to clothe the naked, and to feed the hungry, and to liberate the captive, and administer relief to the sick and the afflicted.

Jacob gives clear and direct advice about what to seek for in life. Although he seems to have a deep intellectual understanding of scripture and doctrine, he is able to give practical advice. In advising his brethren to first seek for the kingdom of God, he shows them that this can be done through earthly means by ministering to others. As we read his words today, we can see how it might be possible for us to be confident that we can find both temporal and spiritual success. The key lies in our hearts. If we possess charity—as we have been commanded, remember—we will serve God and serve others, and in so doing, we will be blessed.

> Jacob 4:7 — Nevertheless, the Lord God showeth us our weakness that we may know that it is by his grace, and his great condescensions unto the children of men, that we have power to do these things.
>
> 8 — Behold, great and marvelous are the works of the Lord. How unsearchable are the depths of the mysteries of him; and it is impossible that man should find out all his ways. And no man knoweth of his ways save it be revealed unto him; wherefore, brethren, despise not the revelations of God.
>
> 9 — For behold, by the power of his word man came upon the face of the earth, which earth was created by the power of his word. Wherefore, if God being able to speak and the world was, and to speak and man was created, O then, why not able to command the earth, or the workmanship of his hands upon the face of it, according to his will and pleasure?
>
> 10 — Wherefore, brethren, seek not to counsel the Lord, but to take counsel from his hand. For behold, ye yourselves know that he counseleth in wisdom, and in justice, and in great mercy, over all his works.

In striving to serve the Lord, to serve others, and to thereby keep our covenants, we often fall short—and we know it. When we know we have fallen short, even though we really wanted to do what is right, we become painfully aware of our weaknesses. Although recognizing our weaknesses can be painful, we should be glad when we do so, for our realization of our weakness is an indication that we have the witness of the Holy Ghost. If we are not aware of our weaknesses, that is a sign that we are on our own, and then our weaknesses may lead to our downfall as Satan makes inroads into our lives.

Jacob contrasts our weakness with the greatness of the Lord, reminding us that because of our weakness, we cannot know the ways of the Lord unless they are revealed to us. We must not, then, despise (or look down upon) the revelations of God, for it is through those revelations—be they recorded in scripture; broadcast in general conference; written in our patriarchal blessings; pronounced upon us in priesthood blessings; or whispered to us by a still, small voice—that we come to know the ways of the Lord. Rather than look down upon the revelations of God, we must rely upon them to find the only sure source of strength that will help us overcome our weaknesses.

In relying upon those revelations to guide us, we seek to follow the counsel of the Lord, rather than trying to impose our own will upon things. Yes, we have agency, but agency is our ability to choose life or death. It is not the freedom to impose our own will upon others or, more importantly, upon ourselves. When we choose to do so, and in so doing choose to take our counsel from the Lord rather than to impose our own will—and weakness—upon the Lord, our neighbors, and ourselves, then we have exercised our agency wisely. And only then will we come to know and appreciate His wisdom, justice, and great mercy.

> Jacob 6:5 — Wherefore, my beloved brethren, I beseech of you in words of soberness that ye would repent, and come with full purpose of heart, and cleave unto God as he cleaveth unto you. And while his arm of mercy is extended towards you in the light of the day, harden not your hearts.

Jacob uses remarkable language when he urges his listeners to cleave unto God as God cleaves unto them. So often in the scriptures we have heard the Lord invite us to come unto him. We have heard the Lord invite us to knock at His door, where He is waiting to receive us. Unfortunately, when we do something that estranges us from Him, rather than immediately try to seek Him out, we seek instead to hide.

Rather than knock at His door in repentance, we hightail it down the road in shame. His arm of mercy is extended toward us, but we often see it as the long arm of the law coming after us. How foolish can we be?

Jacob does go on to talk of justice and judgment in the next several verses, but only to underscore the consequences of failing to seek the mercy of the Lord. He then ends his discourse with an impassioned plea:

> Jacob 6:11 — O then, my beloved brethren, repent ye, and enter in at the strait gate, and continue in the way which is narrow, until ye shall obtain eternal life.
>
> 12 — O be wise; what can I say more?

Indeed, what can Jacob say more? If we are wise, we will seek the Lord. We will seek Him in righteousness to praise him, and we will seek Him in our sin and sorrow to repent and seek for His righteousness, His mercy. To be wise is to seek for the Lord, walking in His path, striving to endure to the end.

> Jacob 7:11 — And I said unto him: Then ye do not understand them; for they truly testify of Christ. Behold, I say unto you that none of the prophets have written, nor prophesied, save they have spoken concerning this Christ.

Reading these words from our contemporary perspective, it may not seem all that startling to hear Jacob declare that all prophets testify of Christ. Our copies of the Book of Mormon declare right on their covers that the Book of Mormon is "another testament of Jesus Christ," and clearly the Doctrine and Covenants, Pearl of Great Price, and New Testament comprise the writings and teaching of prophets who also testified of the Savior.

However, the prophets to whom Jacob was referring are the prophets of what we now call the Old Testament, and in the Old Testament as we have it today, we do not find direct references to Christ. Yes, there are references to a Redeemer to come, a Messiah, and we now know that the Promised Messiah was in fact Jesus of Nazareth, the Christ. The Book of Mormon does an excellent job of showing us that we need to realize that the prophets did indeed prophesy of Christ; that is a major contribution of the book.

> Jacob 7:26 — And it came to pass that I, Jacob, began to be old; and the record of this people being kept on the other plates of Nephi, wherefore, I conclude this record, declaring that I have written according to the best of my knowledge, by saying that the time passed away with us, and also our lives passed away like as it were unto us a dream, we being a lonesome and a solemn people, wanderers, cast out from Jerusalem, born in tribulation, in a wilderness, and hated of our brethren, which caused wars and contentions; wherefore, we did mourn out our days.

Perhaps one of the reasons I have always been so taken by Jacob is that he comes across as such a real human being. Each time I read Jacob's closing lament, I feel a deep sympathy and abiding affection for him. At the same time, though, I am inspired to think that despite his deep-seated loneliness, he reached out to his brethren and stood as a powerful witness. It would have been easy for him to bury himself in the study of scripture and leave ecclesiastical matters in the hands of his brother Nephi, but Jacob did not shirk his duty to his people.

Jacob stood tall as a witness of the Savior. We need to remember Jacob's steadfast example as we read the Book of Mormon and feel blessed by it. We need to share our witness with all of our brothers and sisters.

Chapter 4

Enos through Words of Mormon

The first verse of Enos echoes the very first verse of the Book of Mormon:

> Enos 1:1 — Behold, it came to pass that I, Enos, knowing my father that he was a just man—for he taught me in his language, and also in the nurture and admonition of the Lord—and blessed be the name of my God for it.

Had Enos read Nephi? Reading this verse makes me think he must have spent at least some time thumbing through the plates, as his opening words seem to pay tribute both to his father and to Nephi's writings. Enos then immediately begins to tell us his remarkable story.

> Enos 1:2 — And I will tell you of the wrestle which I had before God, before I received a remission of my sins.

I can recall instances in classes or in talks when someone would recount the story of Enos and his "wrestle with the Lord." Perhaps these people were thinking of the story of Jacob in Genesis, perhaps they were simply not being careful with their language, or perhaps they thought the only way Jacob could obtain forgiveness would be to literally wrestle it from the Lord. In any event, Enos's wrestle was *before* God, not *with* God.

The word *wrestle* is vivid and has strong connotations. What is it to "wrestle"? For many, the meaning of the word has been corrupted by the antics of Hulk Hogan and other such characters. For me, however, the word *wrestle* does not evoke images of huge men engaging in scripted morality plays, involving feather boas and chair-smashing. It is a much more serious business than anything ever promoted by Vince McMahon.

When I was in ninth grade, our high school wrestling coach came over to the junior high to see whether any of us would be interested in trying out for wrestling when we got to high school. To introduce us to the sport and to assess what kind of talent he could expect, he gave us some wrestling lessons and divided our group into weight classes so that we could practice wrestling with each other.

Although you might never believe it to see me now, I was really puny in the ninth grade, so I wound up in the lightest weight class along with two other small classmates. I thought I had a natural talent for wrestling, but that thought did not last for long, as I was repeatedly pinned—laughably easily—by both of my opponents, who were more physically mature and much stronger than I.

The climax of our several weeks of wrestling instruction was a tournament. I already knew I did not have a chance at winning, so I went into what I knew would be my final match, determined to give it my best and not to be pinned.

My opponent immediately got the better of me, and soon had me ready to be pinned. By sheer force of will, I wiggled and grunted and avoided being pinned. It was primal combat. Never in my life had I struggled so hard. Never had I felt so spent.

But I lasted the whole match. As the struggle went on, many of the boys watching were yelling encouragement to me. At times I wanted to give up because I ached so badly and could not get any advantage over my opponent no matter how hard I strained, but I kept wrestling. It seemed as though the match would never end, but finally the coach blew the whistle. My opponent jumped to his feet and then immediately reached down to help me up. Many of my friends were cheering, and the coach ran over and told me I had put up a good fight. I did not score a single point, but I did not get pinned. I was not a winner, but now I really understood what it was to wrestle. To wrestle is to *struggle.*

When I read these opening verses of Enos, I began to realize what a struggle Enos must have had during those hours of agonizing prayer. Then we are told the end result of that struggle:

> Enos 1:5 — And there came a voice unto me, saying: Enos, thy sins are forgiven thee, and thou shalt be blessed.
>
> 6 — And I, Enos, knew that God could not lie; wherefore, my guilt was swept away.

Can you imagine hearing such a pronouncement? But our Lord is a God of mercy, and He has promised us repeatedly that He will forgive our sins if we will but humble ourselves and repent. We may not have such a dramatic tale, but we do know that our sins can be forgiven and our guilt swept away if we will pour our hearts out to Him in humble repentance, as did Enos.

Enos's account of his wrestle before the Lord brings to mind the experience of Joseph Smith. In several of the various accounts of the First Vision, Joseph records that he was told by the Lord that his sins were forgiven. Although the account included in the Pearl of Great Price does not include this specific event, the forgiveness element of the First Vision is alluded to in the Doctrine and Covenants:

> D&C 20:5 — After it was truly manifested unto this first elder that he had received a remission of his sins, he was entangled again in the vanities of the world;
>
> 6 — But after repenting, and humbling himself sincerely, through faith, God ministered unto him by an holy angel, whose countenance was as lightning, and whose garments were pure and white above all other whiteness;

Enos had this experience, Joseph Smith had such an experience, the Apostle Paul had such an experience; indeed, there are many examples in scripture of the dramatic power of the Lord's forgiveness. What is especially memorable about the account of Enos is what he does immediately after hearing the Lord pronounce him forgiven of his sins:

> Enos 1:7 — And I said: Lord, how is it done?

Enos is clearly a young man of great chutzpah! "How is it done?" It is hard to imagine asking the Lord such a question! Perhaps after such a struggle, Enos is still full of spiritual adrenaline. It is almost as if he is still wrestling. But the Lord simply gives him a kind and straightforward answer:

> Enos 1:8. And he said unto me: Because of thy faith in Christ, whom thou hast never before heard nor seen. And many years pass away before he shall manifest himself in the flesh; wherefore, go to, thy faith hath made thee whole.

Not only does Enos have great chutzpah, he also has great faith. We see repeatedly in the Book of Mormon that those who have great faith, and are blessed mightily by the Lord, also tend to have great charity, as evidenced in Enos's case by his subsequent actions.

> Enos 1:9. Now, it came to pass that when I had heard these words I began to feel a desire for the welfare of my brethren, the Nephites; wherefore, I did pour out my whole soul unto God for them.
>
> 10. And while I was thus struggling in the spirit, behold, the voice of the Lord came into my mind again, saying: I will visit thy brethren according to their diligence in keeping my commandments. I have given unto them this land, and it is a holy land; and I curse it not save it be for the cause of iniquity; wherefore, I will visit thy brethren according as I have said; and their transgressions will I bring down with sorrow upon their own heads.

What Enos did immediately after receiving forgiveness may remind us of Lehi. When Lehi tasted the fruit from the tree of life in his vision, he immediately turned his attention to his family. In reading Enos's account, we see that upon obtaining a forgiveness of his sins and a promise of great blessings, Enos's thoughts turn immediately to others, and he prays to the Lord for his brethren. Note how Enos uses another vivid word, "struggling," to characterize his praying. Upon receiving an affirmative answer to his prayer for his brethren, Enos is still not fully satisfied, so he renews his strugglings in a remarkable way.

> Enos 1:11. And after I, Enos, had heard these words, my faith began to be unshaken in the Lord; and I prayed unto him with many long strugglings for my brethren, the Lamanites.

Coming from someone who has prayed mightily to the Lord, obtained a revelation of forgiveness from the Lord, then prayed some more and received more revelation confirming that his prayers would be answered, Enos's assertion that "my faith *began* to be unshaken" seems quite remarkable indeed. Here is one very earnest individual whose talk of wrestling and struggling starts coming into vivid focus.

But not only is Enos an earnest individual, he is also a charitable soul, as demonstrated by his earnest prayer—his "many long strugglings"—on behalf of the Lamanites. Note that he refers to the Lamanites not as his enemies, but as his brethren. After reading less than a dozen verses of his record, it is hard not to be completely taken by this fascinating servant of the Lord. What an example of faith and charity he sets!

There is a lesson to be learned here. We hope that when we obtain a great blessing from the Lord, our first reaction will be one of gratitude. Ideally, we will remember the hand of the Lord and thank Him for the blessing we have received. To do so is commendable.

Still, if we are to truly cultivate charity in our souls, we need to go the extra mile and plead with the Lord to extend blessings to others—and not only to our families, friends, and fellow members of the Church, but also to our enemies. In doing so, we may also realize that the way the Lord extends blessings is through people. If the things with which we have been blessed are to be extended to our families, friends, and enemies, then it will be through us. When we come to have this realization, we will come to have charity, as we have been commanded. The Book of Mormon offers us numerous striking examples of this process.

> Enos 1:12 — And it came to pass that after I had prayed and labored with all diligence, the Lord said unto me: I will grant unto thee according to thy desires, because of thy faith.
>
> 13 — And now behold, this was the desire which I desired of him—that if it should so be, that my people, the Nephites, should fall into transgression, and by any means be destroyed, and the Lamanites should not be destroyed, that the Lord God would preserve a record of my people, the Nephites; even if it so be by the power of his holy arm, that it might be brought forth at some future day unto the Lamanites, that, perhaps, they might be brought unto salvation—
>
> 14 — For at the present our strugglings were vain in restoring them to the true faith. And they swore in their wrath that, if it were possible, they would destroy our records and us, and also all the traditions of our fathers.
>
> 15 — Wherefore, I knowing that the Lord God was able to preserve our records, I cried unto him continually, for he had said unto me: Whatsoever thing ye shall ask in faith, believing that ye shall receive in the name of Christ, ye shall receive it.
>
> 16 — And I had faith, and I did cry unto God that he would preserve the records; and he covenanted with me that he would bring them forth unto the Lamanites in his own due time.
>
> 17 — And I, Enos, knew it would be according to the covenant which he had made; wherefore my soul did rest.
>
> 18 — And the Lord said unto me: Thy fathers have also required of me this thing; and it shall be done unto

> them according to their faith; for their faith was like unto thine.

Note that in verse 12, Enos says "after I had prayed and labored with all diligence," which suggests that there has been a considerable passage of time since his wrestle before the Lord. Having been assured by the Lord that his righteous desires will be granted him, Enos then goes on to ask the Lord—and note that this is expressed in terms of "I cried unto Him continually," which again implies an extended period of time, not a single prayer on any one occasion—that the records of the Nephites would be preserved.

By reading of Enos's devotion to keeping the record and pleading that the record would be preserved, we can reflect that we are benefiting directly from his prayers and diligent labors, for had the record not been preserved, then, of course, we would not be reading it. To some readers, this might be an obvious thought; however, there are times when reflection upon such simple things brings about a profound sense of wonder and gratitude.

> Enos 1:27 — And I soon go to the place of my rest, which is with my Redeemer; for I know that in him I shall rest. And I rejoice in the day when my mortal shall put on immortality, and shall stand before him; then shall I see his face with pleasure, and he will say unto me: Come unto me, ye blessed, there is a place prepared for you in the mansions of my Father. Amen.

In this short chapter, we have seen Enos go from the intense struggle and effort of the first few verses to the remarkable peace and calm of this final verse. Someone who has exhibited the great faith and charity of Enos can expect to be able to "see His face with pleasure." This verse has long struck me as one of the sweetest verses in all of scripture, not just for what it says, but for how it comes as the culmination of an energetic, devoted quest to serve the Lord. Reading it this time suddenly brought to mind another of my favorite sweet scriptures, this one from the Pearl of Great Price:

> Abraham 2:12 — Now, after the Lord had withdrawn

> from speaking to me, and withdrawn his face from me, I said in my heart: Thy servant has sought thee earnestly; now I have found thee;

How I hope and pray that someday I too may come to possess the spiritual assurance felt by Enos and Abraham! For me, though, that day lies further along that strait and narrow path. I am happy, though, to realize that I have a true desire to get to that point. That desire is a great gift from the Lord, a gift without which I would be much the poorer spiritually.

> Jarom 1:1 — Now behold, I, Jarom, write a few words according to the commandment of my father, Enos, that our genealogy may be kept.

"I, Jarom"—genealogist? The son of Enos begins his record with a first-person declaration of identity, then tells us of his desire that the genealogical record be preserved.

> Jarom 1:2 — And as these plates are small, and as these things are written for the intent of the benefit of our brethren the Lamanites, wherefore, it must needs be that I write a little; but I shall not write the things of my prophesying, nor of my revelations. For what could I write more than my fathers have written? For have not they revealed the plan of salvation? I say unto you, Yea; and this sufficeth me.

Jarom tells us that there is no need for him to write about points of doctrine, for the plan of salvation has already been laid out in what has been written previously. From this statement, we can infer that Jarom has been a student of the scriptures and that he has read the plates that were handed down to him by his father.

Having just read of the seriousness of purpose and strength of convictions of Enos, we can further infer that he must have done a thorough job of training his son Jarom in the ways of the Lord before entrusting him with the plates. We also get an inkling that Jarom himself must have been a spiritual man, because he mentions his prophesying and revelations. Not only did Enos face his death with peace in his heart over his standing with the Lord, he must have felt confident that the records would be in good hands with his faithful son.

> Omni 1:1 — Behold, it came to pass that I, Omni, being commanded by my father, Jarom, that I should write somewhat upon these plates, to preserve our genealogy—

"I, Omni"—another genealogist? Omni starts his record the same way his father before him did, but we soon learn that perhaps Jarom did not hand over the record to his son with the same degree of peace and confidence that his father, Enos, handed them over to him.

> Omni 1:2 — Wherefore, in my days, I would that ye should know that I fought much with the sword to preserve my people, the Nephites, from falling into the hands of their enemies, the Lamanites. But behold, I of myself am a wicked man, and I have not kept the statutes and the commandments of the Lord as I ought to have done.

Not often in scripture do we read the writings of self-proclaimed wicked men. Before we rush to judge Omni harshly, though, we might stop to ponder that he tells us that he fought for the freedom of his people. He does so in a way that does not sound as though he is simply trying to justify his sins. Moreover, when we try to form a balanced portrait of Omni in our minds, we must take into account that he is aware that he has not really measured up to the statutes and commandments.

How many of us believe that we have truly kept the statutes and commandments of God as we ought to have done? Probably not very many. How many of us would be willing to write down for public consumption that we have in fact not kept the statutes and commandments of the Lord as we ought to have done? Again, probably not very many. Although not many of us would be likely to describe ourselves as wicked men or women, I believe that most of us know that we have not kept the commandments as well as we ought to have done.

As much as I would love to read the Book of Mormon and see a lot of Nephi or Moroni in myself, I must confess that I see more of Omni, and I cannot add in my own defense, as he did, that "I have fought much to preserve my people." Perhaps that is why it is so sweet to read in the Book of Mormon of the tender mercies of the Lord and of the great plan of happiness that starts with repentance. The very fact that we know that we do not keep the commandments well is what makes the Book of Mormon so compelling to many of us, because it lays so plainly before us the way and the hope of obtaining forgiveness.

> Omni 1:25 — And it came to pass that I began to be old; and, having no seed, and knowing king Benjamin to be a just man before the Lord, wherefore, I shall deliver up these plates unto him, exhorting all men to come unto God, the Holy One of Israel, and believe in prophesying, and in revelations, and in the ministering of angels, and in the gift of speaking with tongues, and in the gift of interpreting languages, and in all things which are good; for there is nothing which is good save it comes from the Lord; and that which is evil cometh from the devil.
>
> 26 — And now, my beloved brethren, I would that ye should come unto Christ, who is the Holy One of Israel, and partake of his salvation, and the power of his redemption. Yea, come unto him, and offer your whole souls as an offering unto him, and continue in fasting and praying, and endure to the end; and as the Lord liveth ye will be saved.

After a line of several keepers of the record who offer only the briefest of comments upon their duties, the records ends up with Amaleki, who offers several verses of significant historical commentary. Amaleki has the spiritual insight to recognize King Benjamin as a righteous soul and to recognize that all good comes from the Lord, and evil from the devil, a theme that appears several times in the Book of Mormon. His capsule summary of the plan of salvation and his straightforward invitation to come unto Christ form a thumbnail portrait of the big picture of salvation presented in the Book of Mormon.

> Words of Mormon 1:7 — And I do this for a wise

> purpose; for thus it whispereth me, according to the workings of the Spirit of the Lord which is in me. And now, I do not know all things; but the Lord knoweth all things which are to come; wherefore, he worketh in me to do according to his will.

As we ponder this verse and try to liken it unto ourselves, we might ask ourselves whether we feel that what we are doing in our lives corresponds to the Lord's purposes. Mormon's declaration, "I do not know all things" is certainly a statement to which we can relate, and many of us also share with Mormon the belief that "the Lord knoweth all things which are to come."

It is that final phrase of this verse that should give us pause. As we liken this scripture unto ourselves, can we reflect seriously upon our lives and discern that the Lord is apparently working in us according to His will? Do we honestly feel that we have consecrated ourselves to the Lord sufficiently that He can bring about His will and purposes through our conscious and sometimes unconscious efforts? Do we pray that His will, not ours be done?

Even when we do not really know what His will is? Or ours?

We must ponder to know our will, we must ponder and pray to know the Lord's will, and we must ponder, pray, and repent to bring our will in line with His. If we do so, He can then work in us and through us according to His will, meaning that He will bless others though us, simultaneously blessing us as we find ourselves by losing ourselves in His service.

Chapter 5

Mosiah

Whenever I read the Book of Mormon, I am always excited to get to Mosiah. Not only does getting there indicate that I am well into the Book of Mormon, but it also means that I am soon going to get to read King Benjamin's address once again. I have often said that if Joseph Smith had brought forth nothing else besides King Benjamin's address, I would have been convinced that he was a prophet of God. What a wonderful sermon this is! It is so densely packed with doctrine that I obviously cannot hope to cover every facet of it. Instead, let me pull out some highlights so we can attempt to liken these doctrines to ourselves and begin to appreciate yet again the wonderful teachings that have been so carefully preserved over the centuries for our benefit.

> Mosiah 2:11 — But I am like as yourselves, subject to all manner of infirmities in body and mind; yet I have been chosen by this people, and consecrated by my father, and was suffered by the hand of the Lord that I should be a ruler and a king over this people; and have been kept and preserved by his matchless power, to serve you with all the might, mind and strength which the Lord hath granted unto me.
>
> 12 — I say unto you that as I have been suffered to

spend my days in your service, even up to this time, and have not sought gold nor silver nor any manner of riches of you;

13 — Neither have I suffered that ye should be confined in dungeons, nor that ye should make slaves one of another, nor that ye should murder, or plunder, or steal, or commit adultery; nor even have I suffered that ye should commit any manner of wickedness, and have taught you that ye should keep the commandments of the Lord, in all things which he hath commanded you—

14 — And even I, myself, have labored with mine own hands that I might serve you, and that ye should not be laden with taxes, and that there should nothing come upon you which was grievous to be borne—and of all these things which I have spoken, ye yourselves are witnesses this day.

15 — Yet, my brethren, I have not done these things that I might boast, neither do I tell these things that thereby I might accuse you; but I tell you these things that ye may know that I can answer a clear conscience before God this day.

16 — Behold, I say unto you that because I said unto you that I had spent my days in your service, I do not desire to boast, for I have only been in the service of God.

17 — And behold, I tell you these things that ye may learn wisdom; that ye may learn that when ye are in the service of your fellow beings ye are only in the service of your God.

King Benjamin begins by telling his people—and us, as we read his account with real intent—that he is like us, subject to weaknesses in both body and mind, but that he has been chosen and set apart to serve. The Lord has directed His servants throughout the ages to serve with all their might, mind, and strength. Once again, we have come across a passage in the Book of Mormon that should cause us to reflect on the principle of consecration, searching our souls to realize that we too have been consecrated by the hand of the Lord to serve him—and

His children—with all our might, mind, and strength.

King Benjamin tells us that in serving others in the Lord's way, we seek not for riches, nor do we seek to impose our will upon others. Rather, we seek to do the Lord's will and further His purposes. We are to follow the commandments of God and encourage others to do the same. If we do these things, serving humbly and energetically, we will learn wisdom, coming to the realization that in serving our fellow beings we are serving the Lord.

The two great commandments direct us to love the Lord and to love our neighbors. To these, King Benjamin offers a corollary—that we are to serve our neighbors and thereby serve our God.

> Mosiah 2:21 — I say unto you that if ye should serve him who has created you from the beginning, and is preserving you from day to day, by lending you breath, that ye may live and move and do according to your own will, and even supporting you from one moment to another—I say, if ye should serve him with all your whole souls yet ye would be unprofitable servants.

Contemplating this verse makes me think of that remarkable phrase of Elder Neal A. Maxwell: "the awful arithmetic of the Atonement." No matter how we add things up, our finite efforts—even taken all together—do not suffice to bridge the infinite gap between imperfection and perfection. It is by grace that we are saved, after all we can do. Even if we look at King Benjamin's assertion in a less metaphysical light, we can see that he is telling us that no matter how much we do to serve the Lord, we will never succeed in doing as much for Him as He has done for us.

If we took that thought at its face value, it might tend to depress us. No matter how much we do, we are still unprofitable servants—so why bother to serve at all? As we continue to read what King Benjamin taught, we begin to receive an answer to this perplexing question.

> Mosiah 2:41 — And moreover, I would desire that ye should consider on the blessed and happy state of those that keep the commandments of God. For behold, they

> are blessed in all things, both temporal and spiritual; and if they hold out faithful to the end they are received into heaven, that thereby they may dwell with God in a state of never-ending happiness. O remember, remember that these things are true; for the Lord God hath spoken it.

The "blessed and happy state" sounds like a great state to visit, but the "state of never-ending happiness" sounds like an even better place to take up permanent residence. If we keep the commandments, Ohio can be a blessed and happy state, as can Utah or California or Baden Wurttemberg, or whatever state in which we might happen to live. What truly counts is not the state where we live, but the state of our faithfulness in keeping the commandments. We see that serving the Lord through serving others and keeping the commandments makes us eligible not just for blessings, but for real happiness, and that through a life of faithful service, we put ourselves in a position to be returned to God and His true happiness.

> Mosiah 3:12 — But wo, wo unto him who knoweth that he rebelleth against God! For salvation cometh to none such except it be through repentance and faith on the Lord Jesus Christ.

Likewise, if we knowingly rebel against God, there will be consequences. King Benjamin has taught us that even though we might serve Him all our days, we are still, in the end, unprofitable servants. Through the Atonement, however, the mercy of the Lord can be extended to us, meaning that we can be forgiven, justified, and sanctified. But if we knowingly rebel against God, our salvation is jeopardized, for salvation is promised only to those who repent and exercise faith in Christ. The importance and centrality of Christ to our salvation is the fundamental doctrine underlying King Benjamin's teachings.

> Mosiah 3:19 — For the natural man is an enemy to God, and has been from the fall of Adam, and will be, forever and ever, unless he yields to the enticings of the Holy Spirit, and putteth off the natural man and becometh a saint through the atonement of Christ the Lord, and becometh

> as a child, submissive, meek, humble, patient, full of love, willing to submit to all things which the Lord seeth fit to inflict upon him, even as a child doth submit to his father.

What is it to be an enemy of God? Does God love His enemies? We have been shown in the Book of Mormon that those who are full of charity, the pure love of Christ, are compelled by the Spirit to love and serve their enemies. Even though the natural man is an enemy to God, the Lord sends forth His Spirit, His word, and His servants to reach out to all and employ patient persuasion in extending to them the opportunity to turn to the Lord. If the Lord will extend patience and hope to those who are His enemies, then surely He will extend love and mercy to those who strive to serve Him, even if they—we—do so unprofitably. When we realize that we serve Him not to profit, but to submit to His will that His will may be done, then we will profit indeed.

> Mosiah 4:1 — And now, it came to pass that when king Benjamin had made an end of speaking the words which had been delivered unto him by the angel of the Lord, that he cast his eyes round about on the multitude, and behold they had fallen to the earth, for the fear of the Lord had come upon them.
>
> 2 — And they had viewed themselves in their own carnal state, even less than the dust of the earth. And they all cried aloud with one voice, saying: O have mercy, and apply the atoning blood of Christ that we may receive forgiveness of our sins, and our hearts may be purified; for we believe in Jesus Christ, the Son of God, who created heaven and earth, and all things; who shall come down among the children of men.
>
> 3 — And it came to pass that after they had spoken these words the Spirit of the Lord came upon them, and they were filled with joy, having received a remission of their sins, and having peace of conscience, because of the exceeding faith which they had in Jesus Christ who should come, according to the words which king Benjamin had spoken unto them.

On this remarkable occasion, the multitude who had assembled to listen to the address of King Benjamin fell to the earth, awakened to a sense of their own sinful state, and appealed to the Lord "with one voice" that the Atonement be applied to them so that they could be forgiven. When we read these verses today, it may well strike us as a bit strange that they all acted as one body and spoke with one voice. We might speculate as to whether this was some sort of manifestation of the Spirit, or whether it may have actually been the result of a preplanned ritual, perhaps some sort of written statement from which they were reading.

Putting aside our questions about the precise mechanism by which they may have acted, we can see that in many ways what they did was not all that strange. Indeed, their attitude of repentance and their appeal to the Lord that the Atonement be applied in their lives is analogous to what Latter-day Saint congregations do each Sunday when they bow their heads and hear a priest appeal to the Lord in their behalf that the effects of the Atonement might be made manifest in their lives.

The multitude that knelt together at the time of King Benjamin did so before the institution of the sacrament by the Lord himself. As far as we know, the sacrament prayers had not yet been revealed. But they obtained a spiritual witness of the remission of their sins, much as we today can obtain a spiritual witness if we partake of the sacrament in an attitude of humility and repentance.

> 4 — And king Benjamin again opened his mouth and began to speak unto them, saying: My friends and my brethren, my kindred and my people, I would again call your attention, that ye may hear and understand the remainder of my words which I shall speak unto you.
>
> 5 — For behold, if the knowledge of the goodness of God at this time has awakened you to a sense of your nothingness, and your worthless and fallen state—
>
> 6 — I say unto you, if ye have come to a knowledge of the goodness of God, and his matchless power, and his wisdom, and his patience, and his long-suffering towards

> the children of men; and also, the atonement which has been prepared from the foundation of the world, that thereby salvation might come to him that should put his trust in the Lord, and should be diligent in keeping his commandments, and continue in the faith even unto the end of his life, I mean the life of the mortal body—
>
> 7 — I say, that this is the man who receiveth salvation, through the atonement which was prepared from the foundation of the world for all mankind, which ever were since the fall of Adam, or who are, or who ever shall be, even unto the end of the world.
>
> 8 — And this is the means whereby salvation cometh. And there is none other salvation save this which hath been spoken of; neither are there any conditions whereby man can be saved except the conditions which I have told you.

In these verses, King Benjamin makes a statement that tends to give us pause when he speaks of his people's "nothingness" and their "worthless and fallen state." These are strong words; indeed, we might well think that King Benjamin is saying "hard things" to his people.

However, we must read carefully and see that King Benjamin has in fact said that "if the knowledge of the goodness of God has awakened you to a sense of your nothingness . . ." He speaks conditionally to point out that this is how his people might feel when they are suddenly made aware of the goodness and matchless power of God. When confronted by that overwhelming reality, we mere mortals might well feel a sense of nothingness in comparison. We are familiar with the finite. When we encounter the infinite, finitude can feel like nothingness in comparison.

King Benjamin goes on to remind his people that through God's goodness and power, through that great atoning sacrifice, the means to their salvation have been established. In that light, King Benjamin then reminds his listeners that it is up to them to keep the conditions under which the benefits of atonement are offered: to keep faith and keep the commandments throughout their mortal lives. Once again we may see an analogy to the sacrament prayers that are uttered today, in which we promise to remember the Lord and keep His commandments.

> Mosiah 4:9 — Believe in God; believe that he is, and that he created all things, both in heaven and in earth; believe that he has all wisdom, and all power, both in heaven and in earth; believe that man doth not comprehend all the things which the Lord can comprehend.

What a powerful admonition is set forth in this verse! We are told first and foremost to believe in God. We are enjoined to recognize and acknowledge that He created all things and to understand that He has all wisdom and power. Furthermore, we are admonished to recognize and acknowledge that human understanding falls short of the Lord's understanding. This admonition is not given to somehow "put us in our place," but rather to show us why we must have faith in the Lord and why we should strive to seek revelation from Him. It also offers us a compelling reason why we should pray and strive to submit to His will and seek that His will, not our will, be done.

> Mosiah 4:16 — And also, ye yourselves will succor those that stand in need of your succor; ye will administer of your substance unto him that standeth in need; and ye will not suffer that the beggar putteth up his petition to you in vain, and turn him out to perish.
>
> 17 — Perhaps thou shalt say: The man has brought upon himself his misery; therefore I will stay my hand, and will not give unto him of my food, nor impart unto him of my substance that he may not suffer, for his punishments are just—
>
> 18 — But I say unto you, O man, whosoever doeth this the same hath great cause to repent; and except he repenteth of that which he hath done he perisheth forever, and hath no interest in the kingdom of God.
>
> 19 — For behold, are we not all beggars? Do we not all depend upon the same Being, even God, for all the substance which we have, for both food and raiment, and for gold, and for silver, and for all the riches which we have of every kind?

I can vaguely recall being impressed by these verses when I first read them as a teenager investigating the Church. But I can quite vividly recall being impressed by these verses when the late Glenn Pearson took us through them in our Honors Book of Mormon course at BYU back in the fall of 1967. I can remember a feeling of electricity going through me as Brother Pearson talked about our obligation to others, even those others whom we are tempted to judge somehow unworthy of our ministrations, in light of King Benjamin's powerful words. Since that lesson, I have felt almost haunted by King Benjamin. "Are we not all beggars?" Those words cut through me still.

Not long before I was called to serve as a bishop, I can recall several instances of being moved nearly to tears by seeing beggars (some of whom were probably not really in great need) on the streets of Columbus, Ohio. Not only did King Benjamin's words come back to me, but I felt as though I was being shown by the Spirit that I must soften my heart. I received the distinct spiritual impression that these poor souls I was encountering, whether genuine beggars or con men, were representative of the wicked world in which we live, a world in which many people live with very little means, hope, or love. As my heart was softened in these experiences, I would then receive a witness that the only real hope for such sufferers was the Atonement of Christ.

Several times I received such a witness, and often I would pray to the Lord to help soften my heart. I knew that the Lord was really trying to teach me something, but the real import of these experiences did not really sink in until I was called as bishop. I then realized that the Lord had been trying to prepare me for this call by softening my heart and making me aware of both the neediness of others and the centrality of the Atonement.

In reading once again these words of King Benjamin, I am struck by the thought that the Atonement was for all—the rich and the poor, the hopeful and hopeless, the saint and the sinner. We cannot begin to suppose that someone cannot be saved through the power of the Atonement; likewise, we ought not even begin to suppose that we have any right to withhold our own substance from any who might stand in need of it.

Mosiah 4:24 — And again, I say unto the poor, ye

> who have not and yet have sufficient, that ye remain from day to day; I mean all you who deny the beggar, because ye have not; I would that ye say in your hearts that: I give not because I have not, but if I had I would give.

This verse makes an impression at several levels. First, it is almost startling to hear the poor being addressed directly in such a manner. We are so used to hearing sermons preached about how the rich have an obligation to the poor that it comes as a bit of a jolt to hear the poor being reminded that this commandment applies to them as well as to the rich.

Next, we realize that even though most of us would characterize ourselves as neither rich nor poor, even those of us in the middle have our obligations. If the rich have obligations, and the poor have obligations, then we in the middle class must surely have obligations, too.

Furthermore, we may begin to realize that this verse actually addresses issues even more fundamental to our salvation than our obligation to help others. It reveals something about the Lord—that He is aware of all of us, whether we are rich, poor, or somewhere in the middle, and that He does not judge us directly by what we give, or by what we do, or by what we say in public, but rather He judges us by what we say in our hearts.

Finally, upon pondering the deeper meanings of this verse, we may begin to realize that we are judged not just on our actions or attitudes toward the beggar, but by that which we say and have in our hearts concerning the Lord. If we draw close to Him with our lips but our hearts are far from him, then we have withheld from Him our most precious offering, the one offering He truly desires: our broken hearts.

> Mosiah 4:27 — And see that all these things are done in wisdom and order; for it is not requisite that a man should run faster than he has strength. And again, it is expedient that he should be diligent, that thereby he might win the prize; therefore, all things must be done in order.

After being reminded so vividly about our obligations to others, we might find ourselves in turmoil, wondering how much we really need to do. Should we sell our cars, downsize our houses, and give all our excess cash away? Should we stop contributing to our 401(k) plan and give all that money as our fast offering donation each month?

Verse 27 offers us some perspective. Even in matters such as helping the poor, we are to act in wisdom and order rather than rushing into hasty judgments about what to do. This does not excuse us from doing anything, nor does it allow us to fall back into our self-centered middle-class disregard of our charitable obligations, but it does encourage us to be diligent and to do things in order. We can work through our families, our quorums, charitable organizations, and other institutions to aid those who need our assistance. We can strive to perform Christlike service by being diligent in performing our home and visiting teaching; by paying a generous fast offering; and by donating time, money, or even blood to charitable organizations. In all these things, we can respond to the challenge issued by King Benjamin in his remarkable sermon.

Will we ever give enough? Will we ever have true charity? We must remember that no matter how much we serve, we will always be unprofitable servants. There is no spreadsheet that will tell us where we stand. Rather than despair that perhaps we have not done enough, we must simply do the best we can and see that the Lord's will, not ours, be done.

> Mosiah 4:29 — And finally, I cannot tell you all the things whereby ye may commit sin; for there are divers ways and means, even so many that I cannot number them.
>
> 30 — But this much I can tell you, that if ye do not watch yourselves, and your thoughts, and your words, and your deeds, and observe the commandments of God, and continue in the faith of what ye have heard concerning the coming of our Lord, even unto the end of your lives, ye must perish. And now, O man, remember, and perish not.

I have always enjoyed sharing these verses with young people. When I served as bishop, I would make it a point once or twice a year to go over these verses with my priests. They would always see the point: there are many ways to sin, but it does us no good to catalog these things or dwell on them. The important thing is to strive to keep the commandments. There are many things of which we can repent, but the important thing is not what we are repenting of, but that we remain repentant.

I sometimes worry that perhaps we tend to spend too much time preaching to our youth about all the things they should not do— break the Word of Wisdom, view pornography, dress immodestly, hang around with the wrong crowd, and so forth—when what we really should be teaching them is repentance and faith in the Lord Jesus Christ, the only way they will be able to free themselves from these sins and transgressions. This is what we need our youth to remember so they will perish not. And what the rest of us need to remember, too, of course.

> Mosiah 5:7 — And now, because of the covenant which ye have made ye shall be called the children of Christ, his sons, and his daughters; for behold, this day he hath spiritually begotten you; for ye say that your hearts are changed through faith on his name; therefore, ye are born of him and have become his sons and his daughters.
>
> 8 — And under this head ye are made free, and there is no other head whereby ye can be made free. There is no other name given whereby salvation cometh; therefore, I would that ye should take upon you the name of Christ, all you that have entered into the covenant with God that ye should be obedient unto the end of your lives.

As we read in these verses of how King Benjamin's people entered into a covenant with the Lord and took upon them the name of Christ, we can reflect on how in our own experience we have done the same. When we are baptized, when we are ordained to the priesthood, when we receive our temple endowment, and when we partake of the sacrament, we are reminded that we have entered into covenants with our God and have taken upon ourselves the name of Christ. We have been made free so that we can choose life over death. Having chosen life and to become His children, we must then press forward and walk in His path unto the end of our lives.

Note the word *unto* in that last phrase of verse 8. It is easy to read over this phrase quickly and think that it says "until the end of your lives." But that is not what it says. It says "unto the end of your lives." (Now, it may simply be that the word *unto* is one of those tiny mistakes in translation. It could be, for example, that Joseph actually did say "until," but his scribe recorded it as "unto.")

Although it may well be that *unto* means exactly what is meant by *until*, I cannot help but interpret *unto* as meaning something stronger than *until. Unto* seems to imply active purpose and striving, while *until* seems simply to denote the passage of time. Perhaps it is not simply that we are counseled to be obedient until the end of our lives, but rather that our very obedience helps shape our lives, giving us a more meaningful end because we have lived with a higher purpose in mind than simply making it to the end.

Yes, I am probably reading way too much into this simple word, but it is fun to give some extra thought to what the Book of Mormon is really telling us. However, we must be careful not to reach beyond the mark. We must only reach until—or unto—we reach the mark.

> Mosiah 11:20 — And it came to pass that there was a man among them whose name was Abinadi; and he went forth among them, and began to prophesy, saying: Behold, thus saith the Lord, and thus hath he commanded me, saying, Go forth, and say unto this people, thus saith the Lord—Wo be unto this people, for I have seen their abominations, and their wickedness, and their whoredoms; and except they repent I will visit them in mine anger.

One of the most fascinating characters in the Book of Mormon is Abinadi. In the past, the main thing I remembered about him was his lecturing the priests of the wicked King Noah, but reading the text this time around, I was suddenly struck by the tone of his calling. The calling of Abinadi shows us a side of the Lord that we would sometimes like to forget.

> Mosiah 11:22 — And it shall come to pass that they shall know that I am the Lord their God, and am a jealous God, visiting the iniquities of my people.

Suddenly we are not reading about a God of mercy, we are reading of "a jealous God." From our previous reading in the Book of Mormon, we know that He is also a merciful God. When we see this side of God being revealed, it is typically in a situation where there has been widespread wickedness among the people.

> Mosiah 11:27. Now when king Noah had heard of the words which Abinadi had spoken unto the people, he was also wroth; and he said: Who is Abinadi, that I and my people should be judged of him, or who is the Lord, that shall bring upon my people such great affliction?

Having read what message Abinadi had been called by the Lord to preach, we should hardly be surprised that King Noah would have a negative reaction. Still, the sheer insolence he displays is remarkable. It is one thing to question the authority of Abinadi, but it is quite another thing altogether to question the authority of the Lord as King Noah does. Surely someone who has surrounded himself with priests, even though those priests may be corrupt, has some knowledge of the Lord.

It seems clear that Noah is not questioning the authority of the Lord from a position of ignorance; instead, this is a form of willful rebellion. When we begin to appreciate the willfulness of this rebellion, then we can also appreciate the tone of Abinadi's calling.

> Mosiah 12:17 — And it came to pass that king Noah caused that Abinadi should be cast into prison; and he commanded that the priests should gather themselves together that he might hold a council with them what he should do with him.
>
> 18 — And it came to pass that they said unto the king: Bring him hither that we may question him; and the king commanded that he should be brought before them.
>
> 19 — And they began to question him, that they

> might cross him, that thereby they might have wherewith to accuse him; but he answered them boldly, and withstood all their questions, yea, to their astonishment; for he did withstand them in all their questions, and did confound them in all their words.
>
> 20 — And it came to pass that one of them said unto him: What meaneth the words which are written, and which have been taught by our fathers, saying:
>
> 21 — How beautiful upon the mountains are the feet of him that bringeth good tidings; that publisheth peace; that bringeth good tidings of good; that publisheth salvation; that saith unto Zion, Thy God reigneth;
>
> 22 — Thy watchmen shall lift up the voice; with the voice together shall they sing; for they shall see eye to eye when the Lord shall bring again Zion;
>
> 23 — Break forth into joy; sing together ye waste places of Jerusalem; for the Lord hath comforted his people, he hath redeemed Jerusalem;
>
> 24 — The Lord hath made bare his holy arm in the eyes of all the nations, and all the ends of the earth shall see the salvation of our God?
>
> 25 — And now Abinadi said unto them: Are you priests, and pretend to teach this people, and to understand the spirit of prophesying, and yet desire to know of me what these things mean?
>
> 26 — I say unto you, wo be unto you for perverting the ways of the Lord! For if ye understand these things ye have not taught them; therefore, ye have perverted the ways of the Lord.
>
> 27 — Ye have not applied your hearts to understanding; therefore, ye have not been wise. Therefore, what teach ye this people?

In these verses we read about the inquisition of Abinadi. The priests asked him questions, intending to cross him up so they could have an excuse for bringing charges against him, but we are not told what those questions were. We are not told how Abinadi answered these questions, nor are we told how many questions he was asked. We are simply told that Abinadi did answer them boldly, to the apparent astonishment of his interrogators. Whatever the questions may have been, they must have been thought to be quite clever by these priests, for it hardly seems that they would have been astonished and confounded by forthright answers to straightforward scriptural or other related religious questions.

The question that we are told about in some detail does not seem to be a question that would be aimed at trying to trip Abinadi up for the purpose of bringing a charge against him. Rather, it seems to have been asked by one of these priests who has actually studied the scriptures. It might well be, then, that having realized that Abinadi is truly inspired of the Lord, this priest is now asking a question to which he actually hopes to get an enlightening answer. Another possible interpretation of this scripture is that the unnamed questioner is mocking Abinadi for his tough talk, while at the same time letting Abinadi know that although his unnamed inquisitor may be a priest for a wicked king, he is not actually as ignorant of the scriptures as he might seem.

Whatever the motivation of his questioner, Abinadi has simply had enough of these questions. He chides the priests of Noah for either not knowing, or knowing and not teaching the ways of the Lord, and declares that they have thus perverted the ways of the Lord. He then observes, "Ye have not applied your hearts to understanding," an observation that I hope does not apply to us as we read the Book of Mormon and other scriptures. Do we honestly apply our hearts to our scripture study? If not, we have not been wise.

To have the law truly written in our hearts, we must truly apply our hearts—not just our minds—to the law. If the words of Christ are to become the law by which we will live, then we must have the words of Christ in our hearts. If we have the words of Christ in our hearts, then we will have charity, the pure love of Christ, in our lives.

> Mosiah 12:33 — But now Abinadi said unto them: I know if ye keep the commandments of God ye shall be saved; yea, if ye keep the commandments which the Lord delivered unto Moses in the mount of Sinai, saying:

> 34 — I am the Lord thy God, who hath brought thee out of the land of Egypt, out of the house of bondage.
>
> 35— Thou shalt have no other God before me.
>
> 36— Thou shalt not make unto thee any graven image, or any likeness of any thing in heaven above, or things which are in the earth beneath.
>
> 37— Now Abinadi said unto them, Have ye done all this? I say unto you, Nay, ye have not. And have ye taught this people that they should do all these things? I say unto you, Nay, ye have not.

The situation has turned around. The inquisition of Abinadi has now become an inquisition by Abinadi. As we read his cutting query, "Have ye done all this?" we might perhaps liken this scripture unto ourselves—have we done all this? Have we taught these things to our people?

> Mosiah 13:11 — And now I read unto you the remainder of the commandments of God, for I perceive that they are not written in your hearts; I perceive that ye have studied and taught iniquity the most part of your lives.

Once again we encounter the phrase "not written in your hearts." Once again we can take the opportunity to reflect on the importance of having the commandments of God written in our hearts.

> Mosiah 13:28 — And moreover, I say unto you, that salvation doth not come by the law alone; and were it not for the atonement, which God himself shall make for the sins and iniquities of his people, that they must unavoidably perish, notwithstanding the law of Moses.

In contemplating this verse in light of the teachings of the Book of Mormon, we can come to see that what is being said is that salvation comes not through just the law, which is written on scrolls and plates, but also through the atonement of Christ, whose law should be written in our hearts.

> Mosiah 15:1 — And now Abinadi said unto them: I

would that ye should understand that God himself shall come down among the children of men, and shall redeem his people.

2 — And because he dwelleth in flesh he shall be called the Son of God, and having subjected the flesh to the will of the Father, being the Father and the Son—

3 — The Father, because he was conceived by the power of God; and the Son, because of the flesh; thus becoming the Father and Son—

4 — And they are one God, yea, the very Eternal Father of heaven and of earth.

5 — And thus the flesh becoming subject to the Spirit, or the Son to the Father, being one God, suffereth temptation, and yieldeth not to the temptation, but suffereth himself to be mocked, and scourged, and cast out, and disowned by his people.

6 — And after all this, after working many mighty miracles among the children of men, he shall be led, yea, even as Isaiah said, as a sheep before the shearer is dumb, so he opened not his mouth.

7 — Yea, even so he shall be led, crucified, and slain, the flesh becoming subject even unto death, the will of the Son being swallowed up in the will of the Father.

8 — And thus God breaketh the bands of death, having gained the victory over death; giving the Son power to make intercession for the children of men—

9 — Having ascended into heaven, having the bowels of mercy; being filled with compassion towards the children of men; standing betwixt them and justice; having broken the bands of death, taken upon himself their iniquity and their transgressions, having redeemed them, and satisfied the demands of justice.

After contending with the corrupt priests and delivering the message of the justice of God and the necessity of keeping God's commandments, Abinadi then exemplifies the mercy of God by offering a beautiful but concise overview of the Atonement. Once again we sense one of the central messages of the Book of Mormon, that the Lord will extend His tender mercies to those who will forsake their sins and follow him.

There is much for us to learn from these words of Abinadi. Not only can we learn about the Atonement by reading what he has to say, but we can also learn that it is not enough to merely contend against evil and preach the law, we must go the extra mile and teach of the Atonement of Jesus Christ. We must not only point out to others their weaknesses, we must also show them where they can find strength. We must not leave them feeling cut off by the law without teaching them about their Divine Redeemer, their Advocate with the Father, so that they can press forward with a steadfastness in Christ and a perfect brightness of hope.

> Mosiah 18:8 — And it came to pass that he said unto them: Behold, here are the waters of Mormon (for thus were they called) and now, as ye are desirous to come into the fold of God, and to be called his people, and are willing to bear one another's burdens, that they may be light;
>
> 9 — Yea, and are willing to mourn with those that mourn; yea, and comfort those that stand in need of comfort, and to stand as witnesses of God at all times and in all things, and in all places that ye may be in, even until death, that ye may be redeemed of God, and be numbered with those of the first resurrection, that ye may have eternal life—
>
> 10 — Now I say unto you, if this be the desire of your hearts, what have you against being baptized in the name of the Lord, as a witness before him that ye have entered into a covenant with him, that ye will serve him and keep his commandments, that he may pour out his Spirit more abundantly upon you?

Countless baptismal talks over the years have referred to the baptismal covenant as found here in Mosiah 18. As we read these words that we have heard so often, we can hear the echo of the two great commandments, to love and serve both God and our neighbors. In verse 10, we can plainly see the outline of the sacrament prayers that are pronounced every Sunday in our sacrament meetings throughout the world. Pondering on these things, we can feel a kinship with our fellow saints both ancient and modern, familiar and unknown.

> Mosiah 23:14 — And also trust no one to be your teacher nor your minister, except he be a man of God, walking in his ways and keeping his commandments.

Reading this verse and hearing Alma saying "trust no one," I smiled to think of Alma as a shadow and type of the X-Files' Agent Mulder; not often have I ever associated Book of Mormon figures with television characters. Whereas Agent Mulder was willing to trust only himself, though, Alma gives us a more positive cautionary word. We must be careful about whom we choose to follow and put our trust in, but we know that we can trust our priesthood leaders as they lead us from, in, and toward righteousness.

> Mosiah 24:13 — And it came to pass that the voice of the Lord came to them in their afflictions, saying: Lift up your heads and be of good comfort, for I know of the covenant which ye have made unto me; and I will covenant with my people and deliver them out of bondage.
>
> 14 — And I will also ease the burdens which are put upon your shoulders, that even you cannot feel them upon your backs, even while you are in bondage; and this will I do that ye may stand as witnesses for me hereafter, and that ye may know of a surety that I, the Lord God, do visit my people in their afflictions.

Here we read of an instance in which the Lord visits His people in their afflictions. How does this relate to us personally? Instead of simply reading this passage to be about something the Lord did in ancient times, we can liken this scripture unto ourselves and take comfort in the knowledge that although the Lord will allow us to have afflictions to try, temper, and strengthen us, we may know of a surety that He will not abandon us in our afflictions. He will remain our strength and our hope if we will exercise faith in His word, repenting of our sins and seeking forgiveness.

Mosiah 26 offers a powerful lesson on the importance of forgiveness and repentance. Hugh Nibley, that great scholar of the Book of Mormon, liked to remark that repentance and forgiveness are the two things that we had to perfect while on earth. Before I served as a bishop, I appreciated his insight on an intellectual level; however, my service as bishop gave me a much deeper appreciation for what Brother Nibley had pointed out to me, for I came to see that repentance and forgiveness are not only absolutely essential for us to learn and practice, but also in doing so—and only in doing so—can we begin to truly know our Savior and thus begin to become humbled and emboldened enough to come unto him.

> Mosiah 26:22 — For behold, this is my church; whosoever is baptized shall be baptized unto repentance. And whomsoever ye receive shall believe in my name; and him will I freely forgive.

Here is another of those verses that I have read many times without giving it much thought. This time around, though, the phrase "baptized unto repentance" suddenly caught my attention and forced me to do some focused reflection.

Over and over we are taught the first principles and ordinances of the gospel: faith, repentance, baptism, and the gift of the Holy Ghost. Over and over we have read the scriptural injunction to repent and be baptized. Our minds begin to settle into a pattern of repentance and then baptism, repentance and then baptism; if we are not careful, we may forget what this verse reminds us, that we are baptized unto repentance.

Yes, we must repent before being baptized, but if anything, it is even more important that we repent after we are baptized. We repent to seek forgiveness, and we gather to partake of the sacrament to witness once again that we have taken upon ourselves the name of Jesus Christ, reminding us of those covenants we made in conjunction with our baptism. As baptized members of the Lord's church, we continually repent, renew our covenants, and try our best to serve the Lord.

Week after week, year after year, the cycle continues. We repent and we renew our baptismal covenants, week after week after week.

We are only baptized once, but we must repent continually, day after day after day, and we continue to repent and partake of the sacrament week after week.

In so doing, we see the larger pattern: repentance, baptism, repentance, forgiveness. We continually seek forgiveness and grant forgiveness. We continually preach repentance and practice repentance. We then begin to see that we truly have been baptized unto repentance.

> Mosiah 26:30 — Yea, and as often as my people repent will I forgive them their trespasses against me.

How often are we forgiven? As often as we repent. Does that give us a license to sin? No—but sin we will, so repent we must.

> Mosiah 26:31 — And ye shall also forgive one another your trespasses; for verily I say unto you, he that forgiveth not his neighbor's trespasses when he says that he repents, the same hath brought himself under condemnation.

How often must we forgive? As often as the opportunity presents itself, and for as long as we live. If we do not forgive, then our repentance will not be accepted. To be forgiven, we must forgive. Forgiveness and repentance are two sides of the same coin. If we are indeed baptized unto repentance, then we are baptized unto forgiveness. Repent and be baptized. Repent and be forgiven. Forgive and be repentant. Preach repentance and practice forgiveness—and practice what you preach.

> Mosiah 27:25 — And the Lord said unto me: Marvel not that all mankind, yea, men and women, all nations, kindreds, tongues and people, must be born again; yea, born of God, changed from their carnal and fallen state, to a state of righteousness, being redeemed of God, becoming his sons and daughters;
>
> 26 — And thus they become new creatures; and unless they do this, they can in nowise inherit the kingdom of God.

Among Latter-day Saints there has been a reticence to speak of being born again, but certainly the Book of Mormon reminds us that we must indeed become "born again . . . new creatures" if we are to inherit the Kingdom of God. Perhaps what has kept us from describing ourselves as "born again" is our knowledge through modern revelation that to become born again is a necessary, but not sufficient condition for salvation. We must become born again to enter the strait and narrow path, but then we must endure to the end, making and keeping essential covenants, and observing essential ordinances to obtain eternal life through the atoning power and mercy of our Lord.

> Mosiah 28:1 — Now it came to pass that after the sons of Mosiah had done all these things, they took a small number with them and returned to their father, the king, and desired of him that he would grant unto them that they might, with these whom they had selected, go up to the land of Nephi that they might preach the things which they had heard, and that they might impart the word of God to their brethren, the Lamanites—
>
> 2 — That perhaps they might bring them to the knowledge of the Lord their God, and convince them of the iniquity of their fathers; and that perhaps they might cure them of their hatred towards the Nephites, that they might also be brought to rejoice in the Lord their God, that they might become friendly to one another, and that there should be no more contentions in all the land which the Lord their God had given them.

When reading about the mission of the sons of Mosiah, it is hard not to think of Enos, who upon being blessed by the Lord prayed for the spiritual welfare of his brethren, the Lamanites. We have seen and will continue to see this pattern in the Book of Mormon: receiving a great blessing and then demonstrating charity by reaching out toward those who have strayed.

> Mosiah 29:12. Now it is better that a man should be judged of God than of man, for the judgments of God are always just, but the judgments of man are not always just.

Here is a verse that makes me want to shout "Amen!" Still, there are times when we can fool our fellow men and women, and be judged by them better than we deserve; however, even though we cannot fool God, deep in our hearts we know that it is His judgment that really counts. If we are on the strait and narrow path, then we should not fear His judgment. If we are not on that path, then we should exercise our own judgment and get back on it.

CHAPTER 6

Alma

When I am reading the Book of Mormon and get to Alma, I feel as though I am making great progress. Then it hits me—Alma is by far the largest book in the Book of Mormon, and I am not yet even halfway done. I have climbed the foothills only to discover a great peak still looming before me. Onward and upward!

> Alma 1:3 — And he had gone about among the people, preaching to them that which he termed to be the word of God, bearing down against the church; declaring unto the people that every priest and teacher ought to become popular; and they ought not to labor with their hands, but that they ought to be supported by the people.

Suddenly a new preacher appears on the scene. His teaching about the role of the priesthood seems to be quite removed from the teaching of King Benjamin. However, his teaching about salvation seems, at least on first encounter, to be quite appealing:

> Alma 1:4 — And he also testified unto the people that all mankind should be saved at the last day, and that they need not fear nor tremble, but that they might lift up their heads and rejoice; for the Lord had created all men, and had also redeemed all men; and, in the end, all men should have eternal life.

What's wrong with this doctrine? After all, it invites us to "lift up our heads and rejoice," it teaches us that we were created by the Lord, and it testifies that He has redeemed all men. Indeed, the phrase "all men should have eternal life," certainly seems to be in harmony with the phrase uttered by the Lord himself in Moses 1:39, "This is my work and my glory, to bring to pass the immortality and eternal life of man." We often teach in the Church that the infinite Atonement was a universal sacrifice for all sins. We also invite all to come unto Christ, who, we teach, will turn away none who come unto him.

This preaching of Nehor is appealing doctrine, and it seems to have some resonance with true teaching. It seems to have been fairly well-received among the Nephites. However, it is important that we understand precisely what is wrong with it.

My experience in teaching the Book of Mormon is that when I ask students to explain just what is wrong with this particular verse, especially after I have spent a little time pointing out its similarities to true doctrine, many of them hesitate to respond. Part of their hesitation seems to be because they had automatically dismissed the teachings of Nehor because (a) they had always been taught that Nehor was an anti-Christ and (b) Nehor's obvious profit motive makes it seem clear that he is a false teacher; however, they had never really given much thought to what was actually wrong with his doctrinal pronouncements about the nature of salvation.

Thankfully, there are a few students who have already thought this through. They see right away that Christ did not teach that all *would* be saved, only that all *could* be saved if they would but repent and come unto him. By leaving this important condition out of his account, Nehor was able to fashion a doctrine with undeniable popular appeal, which he exploited for all it was worth and then some.

> Alma 1:5 — And it came to pass that he did teach these things so much that many did believe on his words, even so many that they began to support him and give him money.
>
> 6 — And he began to be lifted up in the pride of his

> heart, and to wear very costly apparel, yea, and even began to establish a church after the manner of his preaching.

Using his false teaching, Nehor starts turning a profit. For many, the good news is that you can buy anything in this world for money.

> Alma 1:15 — And it came to pass that they took him; and his name was Nehor; and they carried him upon the top of the hill Manti, and there he was caused, or rather did acknowledge, between the heavens and the earth, that what he had taught to the people was contrary to the word of God; and there he suffered an ignominious death.

The bad news for Nehor is that the kingdom of heaven is not of this world, and salvation cannot be bought—or sold for a profit. He finds out too late that, as the song goes, "money changes everything." Had Nehor been content merely to teach false doctrine, he may have had a moderately successful career. But when he let pride consume him, he soon paid the price himself, a far greater price than he had ever imagined.

> Alma 1:17 — Nevertheless, they durst not lie, if it were known, for fear of the law, for liars were punished; therefore they pretended to preach according to their belief; and now the law could have no power on any man for his belief.

As we read this verse and see that liars were punished by law, our minds may well be drawn back to the Ten Commandments, wherein we are, among other things, commanded not to bear false witness. As we read that "the law could have no power on any man for his belief," and we see how they tried to avoid the law by pretending (or, in other words, lying) to preach according to their belief, we can see what a deceptive pattern of manipulation was being established by those who followed Nehor's teachings.

If we examine our own lives closely, however, we will no doubt recall instances where for one reason or another—some good, some bad—we have "pretended to preach" according to our belief. For example, we may have bitten our tongues when asked if there was anything bothering us, because we were afraid of hurting someone's feelings. Or we may have given a sacrament meeting talk wherein we stressed the importance of daily scripture study, when in reality it was something about which we were not fully convinced and did not really practice.

As we reflect on such blemishes on our own character, we may feel relief that at least our laws today also let us be free in our beliefs, letting us work out problems without coercion. Even in the Church, we are generally free to say what we believe, or at least what we pretend to believe. If we get up to the pulpit and advocate daily scripture study even though we do not actually practice it, chances are excellent that we are not going to get called on it by our bishop.

Still, as we read this verse, we recognize that people are certainly not justified by pretending to preach according to their belief. As we reflect upon our own shortcomings in this regard, we may come to realize that we have fallen short and thus have great need of repentance. The law may let us slide, the bishop may pay us no mind, but the Lord will not be fooled—and we know it.

> Alma 1:21 — Now there was a strict law among the people of the church, that there should not any man, belonging to the church, arise and persecute those that did not belong to the church, and that there should be no persecution among themselves.

Reading this verse, I am led to reflect on how Joseph Smith taught religious tolerance and to be appreciative that our church does not teach against other churches. This is especially remarkable when you think of the persecution we have endured, and how we have taught that our Church is the only true and living Church. It can be a delicate balancing act—on one hand to maintain that you are a member of the true Church, and on the other hand respect the beliefs of others. Except for a few older and crankier high priests, who occasionally seem to offer some strange characterizations of other religions from time to time, I have always found it remarkable how tolerant our members seem to be.

> Alma 3:19 — Now I would that ye should see that they brought upon themselves the curse; and even so doth every man that is cursed bring upon himself his own condemnation.

As I read this verse I think not about the Lamanites; I think about myself. There have been times in my life when I have felt cursed, or under a condemnation, but I must concede that upon reflection, I really had brought it on myself. I could not blame the Lord, although there were times when I did blame the Church. Deep down, however, I knew that I would be happier were I more diligent in keeping the commandments. There were times when I characterized myself as not a religious person; in truth, the problem was that I was not a repentant person.

> Alma 3:27 — For every man receiveth wages of him whom he listeth to obey, and this according to the words of the spirit of prophecy; therefore let it be according to the truth. And thus endeth the fifth year of the reign of the judges.

Who signs our paychecks? We need to ask ourselves that question from time to time. It is a question that goes back to the days of Cain and Abel and continues to be relevant today.

> Alma 4:19 — And this he did that he himself might go forth among his people, or among the people of Nephi, that he might preach the word of God unto them, to stir them up in remembrance of their duty, and that he might pull down, by the word of God, all the pride and craftiness and all the contentions which were among his people, seeing no way that he might reclaim them save it were in bearing down in pure testimony against them.

"Bearing down in pure testimony" is a concept and a practice with great spiritual power. Beyond argument, beyond persuasion, relying wholly on the Spirit, pure testimony is strong to save. The Savior bore down in pure testimony when He read Messianic prophecy from Isaiah and then told those assembled in the synagogue, "This day is this scripture fulfilled in your ears" (see Luke 4:18–21).

Another scriptural instance of bearing down in pure testimony, this from the early days of the Restoration, is recorded in Section 76 of the Doctrine and Covenants: "And now, after the many testimonies which have been given of him, this is the testimony, last of all, which we give of him: That he lives! For we saw him, even on the right hand of God; and we heard the voice bearing record that he is the Only Begotten of the Father—That by him, and through him, and of him, the worlds are and were created, and the inhabitants thereof are begotten sons and daughters unto God" (D&C 76:22–24). It is hard to read those words without feeling spiritually overwhelmed.

For the Saints of my generation, though, perhaps the most memorable words of pure testimony were those uttered by Elder Bruce R. McConkie in his final General Conference address, shortly before he passed away: "I am one of His witnesses, and in a coming day I shall feel the nail marks in His hands and in His feet and shall wet His feet with my tears. But I shall not know any better then than I know now that He is God's Almighty Son, that He is our Savior and Redeemer, and that salvation comes in and through His atoning blood and in no other way"[1]

These three brief but powerful examples I have given are examples of what Alma was getting at when he wrote of the reclaiming power of bearing down in pure testimony. It is something that missionaries need to do as they labor to bring souls to Christ, and it is something that parents need to do to reclaim their precious children.

All of us, in fact, need to examine ourselves and find out what we can witness in pure testimony. If we are lacking, we can pray, "Lord, I believe—help me in my unbelief."

> Alma 5:3 — I, Alma, having been consecrated by my father, Alma, to be a high priest over the church of God, he having power and authority from God to do these things, behold, I say unto you that he began to establish a church in the land which was in the borders of Nephi; yea, the

> land which was called the land of Mormon; yea, and he did baptize his brethren in the waters of Mormon.

Here is another example of a speaker in the Book of Mormon beginning his discourse by establishing his ecclesiastical authority. In this instance, Alma not only lays out his own claim to authority, but also lays out the authority of the Church, so that when he speaks to members of the Church, he can remind them of their spiritual obligations, much as our Church leaders often do today when they remind us of the restoration of the priesthood power and authority that underlies our baptismal and temple covenants.

> Alma 5:6 — And now behold, I say unto you, my brethren, you that belong to this church, have you sufficiently retained in remembrance the captivity of your fathers? Yea, and have you sufficiently retained in remembrance his mercy and long-suffering towards them? And moreover, have ye sufficiently retained in remembrance that he has delivered their souls from hell?

Today, we are not as likely to hear about our "fathers in captivity" (although, we often hear the story of Joseph Smith in Liberty Jail), but we are often asked to remember the persecutions of our pioneer forebears and the mercy shown to them by the Lord. We don't often hear how the Lord delivered their souls from hell; rather, we hear of how He has reserved a place for them in His eternal kingdom. Clearly, though, this is a scripture we can liken to ourselves, reflecting on the goodness and mercy of the Lord and how such accounts help sustain our faith in His mercy in our present predicament. We all need the help of the Lord. Knowing that the Lord heard the prayers of our fathers in the past gives us faith that He will hear our prayers today and in the future.

> Alma 5:12 — And according to his faith there was a mighty change wrought in his heart. Behold I say unto you that this is all true.

Most of us remember the phrase "mighty change of heart" as

found in the Book of Mormon, and many of us no doubt remember that the story is found in Alma. It is instructive to read the story once again with fresh eyes and suddenly see what had been there all along: that Alma prefaces the story with the observation that faith brings the mighty change. To paraphrase the title of that famous book by President Kimball, we might say that "faith precedes the mighty change."

> Alma 5:14 — And now behold, I ask of you, my brethren of the church, have ye spiritually been born of God? Have ye received his image in your countenances? Have ye experienced this mighty change in your hearts?

These are penetrating questions that we need to ask ourselves as we read these verses. Do you feel as though you have indeed been born again? Have you been spiritually born of God? When you look in the mirror, do we see the image of a son or daughter of God? Have you received His image in your countenance? Do you know that your life has truly been changed for the better by your faith in the Lord? Have you experienced this mighty change in your heart?

> Alma 5:15 — Do ye exercise faith in the redemption of him who created you? Do you look forward with an eye of faith, and view this mortal body raised in immortality, and this corruption raised in incorruption, to stand before God to be judged according to the deeds which have been done in the mortal body?

Note well that Alma does not ask whether we *have* faith, but whether we *exercise* faith in our Creator. Remember, he has taught that faith precedes the mighty change, but now we can see that this must be active faith, not merely passive belief. Those who exercise faith inspire hope and practice charity. Those who practice charity and have the pure love of Christ in their hearts and the image of God in their countenances can indeed look forward to their eventual judgment with an eye of faith.

> Alma 5:16 — I say unto you, can you imagine to yourselves that ye hear the voice of the Lord, saying unto you, in that day: Come unto me ye blessed, for behold, your works have been the works of righteousness upon the face of the earth?

This is a sweet scripture. You can feel its persuasive power as you find yourself imagining that at the end of your earthly life, the Lord would personally offer such an invitation to you. It makes you want to be obedient, to be faithful and true, to endure to the end.

This is also a fascinating scripture in how it offers a positive instance of rhetoric. As a former speech teacher and rhetoric major, I see in this scripture not just an appeal to doctrine, but a clever use of rhetoric for a righteous purpose (Hugh Nibley, one of my intellectual heroes, especially regarding the Book of Mormon, used to love to beat up on rhetoric, so it is especially satisfying to discover a positive example of rhetoric right in the Book of Mormon).

Note the language: "Can you imagine?" (a contrast to the usual Book of Mormon question, "Do you remember?"). One of the rhetorical devices we used to teach our speech students was the Monroe Motivated Sequence, a method for organizing a persuasive presentation that derived its power to persuade from having the speaker employ what Monroe called "the visualization step." This step asked the audience to do just what Alma is doing here, that is, to imagine themselves in a highly appealing (or extremely unappealing, if the intent of the speech were negative) situation so they realize that by applying whatever it is the speaker is trying to persuade them to do, they can achieve that goal. We may say in our hearts, "I want to be welcomed by the Savior when I stand before Him in that day and I can imagine how wonderful that would be; so yes, I really do want to repent and keep His commandments. As difficult as that might be, I know that it will be more than worth it."

> Alma 5:26 — And now behold, I say unto you, my brethren, if ye have experienced a change of heart, and if ye have felt to sing the song of redeeming love, I would ask, can ye feel so now?

Just what is "the song of redeeming love"? Have you ever sung it? I have sung it, many times. I'll bet you have sung it too, but perhaps you did not realize that is what you were doing at the time.

For me, sacrament hymns are songs of redeeming love, especially when I sing them sincerely, truly reflecting on the Atonement of Christ. "How Firm a Foundation" is a hymn I find to be a song of redeeming love, as is "Where Can I Turn for Peace?" Of course, there are many songs of redeeming love; as we sing them sincerely, the Lord has promised they will be a prayer unto Him. Just reflecting on these promises makes us want to sing these songs of redeeming love again—"can ye feel so now?"

> Alma 5:28 — Behold, are ye stripped of pride? I say unto you, if ye are not ye are not prepared to meet God. Behold ye must prepare quickly; for the kingdom of heaven is soon at hand, and such an one hath not eternal life.

For most Latter-day Saints of my generation, this scripture brings to mind the great conference address on pride, by President Ezra Taft Benson (although I have found that many of my generation have forgotten that the address was actually not delivered by President Benson himself. It was read in the opening session of the April 1989 general conference by President Gordon B. Hinckley). To make his central message clear, President Benson employed simple language and the straightforward rhetorical device of repetition: "Pride is the great stumbling block to Zion. I repeat: Pride is the great stumbling block to Zion."

Another thing that this scripture brings to mind is another, more frequently quoted scripture that says, as any good seminary student can tell us, "This life is the time for men to prepare to meet God" (Alma 34:32). Thinking logically about these two scriptures, we can readily conclude that taken together, they teach us that this life is the time for us to strip ourselves of pride. We must learn to forgive, to repent, and to humble ourselves. The longer we live, the more we may come to realize that in order to forgive or to repent, we must first humble ourselves. In other words, we must first strip ourselves of pride.

> Alma 5:33 — Behold, he sendeth an invitation unto all men, for the arms of mercy are extended towards them, and he saith: Repent, and I will receive you.

Nehor had taught that all would be saved, which was not quite right. However, the invitation to salvation is indeed extended to all. The condition attached is repentance.

> Alma 5:38 — Behold, I say unto you, that the good shepherd doth call you; yea, and in his own name he doth call you, which is the name of Christ; and if ye will not hearken unto the voice of the good shepherd, to the name by which ye are called, behold, ye are not the sheep of the good shepherd.

The name by which we are called to be saved is the name of Christ. We must be willing to take the name of Christ upon us, as King Benjamin taught. We affirm our willingness to do so when we partake of the sacrament, when we participate in temple ordinances, and when we strive to serve him. As we do so, we not only take His name upon us, but we begin, through the Spirit, to be more like Him. The sheep become even as the Lamb as they are born again.

> Alma 5:52 — And again I say unto you, the Spirit saith: Behold, the ax is laid at the root of the tree; therefore every tree that bringeth not forth good fruit shall be hewn down and cast into the fire, yea, a fire which cannot be consumed, even an unquenchable fire. Behold, and remember, the Holy One hath spoken it.

The image of the tree is prevalent in the Book of Mormon, being used to depict both the good (the Tree of Life from Lehi and Nephi's dreams) and the wicked, as in this verse. What is particularly striking about this verse is the phrase "unquenchable fire," a phrase that lingers in the memory, reinforced by the assertion that "the Holy One hath spoken it." Truly, we ought to examine ourselves and make sure that we will be counted among those trees that bring forth good fruit.

> Alma 5:54 — Yea, will ye persist in supposing that ye are better one than another; yea, will ye persist in the persecution of your brethren, who humble themselves and do walk after the holy order of God, wherewith they have been brought into this church, having been sanctified by the Holy Spirit, and they do bring forth works which are meet for repentance—
>
> 55 — Yea, and will you persist in turning your backs upon the poor, and the needy, and in withholding your substance from them?

"Will ye persist?" is a cutting question. It does not merely point out that there has been sin, but that the sin has become willful and deliberate. Those being accused have not simply turned their backs against the poor without thinking, as all of us have probably done from time to time, but have let themselves become the kinds of people who continually and deliberately turn their backs against the poor. They are not being judged just for what they do, but for what they are. It may not be that hard to repent of things that we have done foolishly, without thinking, but it is another matter entirely to repent of having become that which we ought not to be—habitual or even hardened sinners.

> Alma 5:61 — And now I, Alma, do command you in the language of him who hath commanded me, that ye observe to do the words which I have spoken unto you.
>
> 62 — I speak by way of command unto you that belong to the church; and unto those who do not belong to the church I speak by way of invitation, saying: Come and be baptized unto repentance, that ye also may be partakers of the fruit of the tree of life.

Sometimes, scriptures that do not overtly address doctrinal themes can be shown, upon closer inspection, to be rich in doctrinal material, scriptures that can teach us valuable gospel lessons. For example, Alma says that he commands "in the language of Him who hath commanded me." Without directly referring to Christ, Alma invokes the authority of Christ. He also teaches of Christ; specifically, that Christ commands—not simply suggests, or entreats, or recommends—that we observe His commandments. That may seem like a simple and obvious point—tautological, even—but there are those who have not learned that simple lesson.

As we reflect further on these verses, we can see a double layer of meaning: first, Alma is commanding that his hearers observe that which he has taught them; second, Christ has commanded Alma to observe those things that he has spoken to Alma. We might further find ourselves reflecting on the idea that in so framing his words, Alma is also implying that the things he has taught are those things that the Lord has revealed to him.

Another interesting principle to observe in pondering these verses is how Alma says that he speaks by way of commandment in speaking to the members of the Church, exercising his priesthood authority, while to those who are not members of the Church, he speaks by way of invitation. Note that Alma here employs the phrase that was used by the Lord back in Mosiah 26:22, "baptized unto repentance." By being baptized unto repentance, and then living repentantly, we are promised that we can partake of the fruit (the Resurrection and the Atonement) of the tree of life (Christ).

Finally, we might observe that in these two verses we are taught that although we are invited to come to Christ through baptism, once we do so, and become members of His church, then we are under commandment—not just invitation—to live according to His teachings. The covenant of baptism is serious business that puts members of the Church under solemn obligation. It also promises great blessings for those whose baptism is truly "unto repentance."

> Alma 6:6 — Nevertheless the children of God were commanded that they should gather themselves together oft, and join in fasting and mighty prayer in behalf of the welfare of the souls of those who knew not God.

Once again we see the theme of those who have been greatly blessed by the Lord praying for the welfare of others. In this verse we see that they do not just pray individually, but are commanded to gather themselves together in fasting and prayer. We read that these blessed souls are referred to as "the children of God."

In our day we also know that we are the children of God. We know that we are still commanded to gather together often to fast and pray on behalf of those who do not yet know the Lord. This happens in our temples, our chapels, and our homes.

> Alma 7:7 — For behold, I say unto you there be many things to come; and behold, there is one thing which is of more importance than they all—for behold, the time is not far distant that the Redeemer liveth and cometh among his people.

Here is another verse that we see echoed in our day. Today, as then, the most important thing is that the Redeemer still lives and will come among His people. We have faith that Christ will return triumphant to rule and reign with His people. The work we do today as missionaries and temple workers is in preparation for that great day.

> Alma 7:11 — And he shall go forth, suffering pains and afflictions and temptations of every kind; and this that the word might be fulfilled which saith he will take upon him the pains and the sicknesses of his people.
>
> 12 — And he will take upon him death, that he may loose the bands of death which bind his people; and he will take upon him their infirmities, that his bowels may be filled with mercy, according to the flesh, that he may know according to the flesh how to succor his people according to their infirmities.

The philosopher Thomas Hobbes famously described what he called the condition of man in the "state of Nature" as "solitary, poor, nasty, brutish, and short." One of Buddha's central tenets was that "life is suffering." In this telestial world in which we find ourselves, we truly are beset with pains and afflictions and temptations of every kind. This is the condition that our God took upon himself in coming to the earth to live as we live, in the flesh. If that were not enough, He then, through some process that we cannot fully comprehend, took upon

Himself in the Garden of Gethsemane not just the typical infirmities and pain that we all face, but all pain and all infirmities. Beyond even these formidable burdens, He took on death itself; not only His death, but our deaths—all death.

If we have not done so previously in our reading of the Book of Mormon, then we should at least look back to our other scriptures to see what is meant by the statement "that the word might be fulfilled which saith He will take upon Him the pains and sicknesses of His people." In the New Testament, for example, Jesus declared about His own mission that:

> Luke 4:18 — The Spirit of the Lord is upon me, because he hath anointed me to preach the gospel to the poor; he hath sent me to heal the brokenhearted, to preach deliverance to the captives, and recovering of sight to the blind, to set at liberty them that are bruised,

And in so doing, He was reflecting upon and announcing the fulfillment of the prophecy of Isaiah:

> Isaiah 61:1 — The Spirit of the Lord God is upon me; because the Lord hath anointed me to preach good tidings unto the meek; he hath sent me to bind up the brokenhearted, to proclaim liberty to the captives, and the opening of the prison to them that are bound;
>
> 2 — To proclaim the acceptable year of the Lord, and the day of vengeance of our God; to comfort all that mourn;
>
> 3 — To appoint unto them that mourn in Zion, to give unto them beauty for ashes, the oil of joy for mourning, the garment of praise for the spirit of heaviness; that they might be called trees of righteousness, the planting of the Lord, that he might be glorified.

As we read in these verses of the desire of the Lord to succor His people, and reflect upon the thought that the Lord came down to dwell among us and take upon himself pain and temptation and even death itself so He might conquer these things not just for Himself, but for all of us, we once again can feel our souls being stirred as we confront and contemplate the mercy and goodness of our Lord. The Book of Mormon is such a powerful witness of the Atonement!

> Alma 7:14 — Now I say unto you that ye must repent, and be born again; for the Spirit saith if ye are not born again ye cannot inherit the kingdom of heaven; therefore come and be baptized unto repentance, that ye may be washed from your sins, that ye may have faith on the Lamb of God, who taketh away the sins of the world, who is mighty to save and to cleanse from all unrighteousness

Once again this basic tenet is proclaimed: we must repent and be born again, and be baptized unto repentance. This latter phrase, upon which we have previously reflected, is surely one of the pearls of great price to be found in the Book of Mormon. If we learn nothing else from our reading of the Book of Mormon other than that baptism is unto repentance, we shall have learned something very important indeed. Of course, there is so much more to be learned and to be treasured. The Book of Mormon is a string of pearls.

> Alma 7:15 — Yea, I say unto you come and fear not, and lay aside every sin, which easily doth beset you, which doth bind you down to destruction, yea, come and go forth, and show unto your God that ye are willing to repent of your sins and enter into a covenant with him to keep his commandments, and witness it unto him this day by going into the waters of baptism.

Here we can see the nucleus of the sacrament prayers that we listen to each week when we witness to the Lord, as we did at our baptism, that we have entered into a covenant to keep His commandments. We are also reminded that unless we do repent of our sins, they will eventually bind us down to destruction. We are free to choose life over death.

> Alma 7:20 — I perceive that it has been made known unto you, by the testimony of his word, that he cannot walk in crooked paths; neither doth he vary from that which he

> hath said; neither hath he a shadow of turning from the right to the left, or from that which is right to that which is wrong; therefore, his course is one eternal round.

The phrase "one eternal round," used to describe the path of the Lord, appears in many places in the scriptures. For us, though, the path is said to be straight and laid out before us. We too are not to turn to the left or the right, nor to turn from that which is right toward that which is wrong. As we progress though life and look both back on where we have been and forward to where we are going—from spirit world to mortality to the world of spirit once again, from young to old to young once again—perhaps we will begin to see our own lives beginning to trace a circle. For now, however, the important thing for us is to keep pressing forward, whether we see our path as ultimately straight or round.

> Alma 7:23 — And now I would that ye should be humble, and be submissive and gentle; easy to be entreated; full of patience and long-suffering; being temperate in all things; being diligent in keeping the commandments of God at all times; asking for whatsoever things ye stand in need, both spiritual and temporal; always returning thanks unto God for whatsoever things ye do receive.
>
> 24 — And see that ye have faith, hope, and charity, and then ye will always abound in good works.

Alma here offers some solid and plain advice that will help us to press forward along the proper path in life. We are to be quick to ask for what we need and quick to return thanks for that with which we are blessed. But in other things, we are to be humble, submissive, and patient. Too many times we find ourselves being just the opposite: proud, assertive, and impatient. We are often too independent to ask for help, even when we need it, and slow even to recognize—much less to acknowledge and be grateful for—the blessings of the Lord.

> Alma 10:6 — Nevertheless, I did harden my heart, for I was called many times and I would not hear; therefore I knew concerning these things, yet I would not

> know; therefore I went on rebelling against God, in the wickedness of my heart, even until the fourth day of this seventh month, which is in the tenth year of the reign of the judges.

Amulek says of himself that he was called but would not hear, that he knew but "would not know." Can we relate to this ambiguity? There have certainly been times in my own life that I knew, "yet I would not know." And yes, those were the times in my life when my heart was hard, for I had hardened it, and had done so deliberately. Looking back, I can see that it was a hard way to live. Not only was it hard for me, it was hard for those who loved me. To have a soft heart is better for all concerned.

> Alma 10:27 — And now behold, I say unto you, that the foundation of the destruction of this people is beginning to be laid by the unrighteousness of your lawyers and your judges.
>
> 32 — Now the object of these lawyers was to get gain; and they got gain according to their employ.

One way to look at these verses is to see them as saying that flaws and corruption in the legal system will inevitably lead to problems and failures in society itself. This is certainly a reasonable interpretation. However, we can also look deeper and see other interpretations to formulate.

For example, we can ask ourselves whether the problem of unrighteous lawyers and judges was the central problem that would lead the Nephites to destruction, or whether the unrighteousness of the lawyers and judges was in itself rather a symptom of a deeper problem. We might reflect on the many examples in the scriptures where the desire for gain is symptomatic of a heart that has been hardened, where the two great commandments—to love God and to love our neighbor—have been superseded by the desire to magnify self. This deep-rooted spiritual problem leads to unrighteous desires and greed, which in turn lead to attitudes and behaviors that can undermine a whole society or people. Corrupt lawyers and judges are not just a secular, societal problem for the Nephites, they are evidence of deeper problems in the hearts and minds of the Nephite people themselves.

> Alma 11:43 — The spirit and the body shall be reunited again in its perfect form; both limb and joint shall be restored to its proper frame, even as we now are at this time; and we shall be brought to stand before God, knowing even as we know now, and have a bright recollection of all our guilt.
>
> 44 — Now, this restoration shall come to all, both old and young, both bond and free, both male and female, both the wicked and the righteous; and even there shall not so much as a hair of their heads be lost; but every thing shall be restored to its perfect frame, as it is now, or in the body, and shall be brought and be arraigned before the bar of Christ the Son, and God the Father, and the Holy Spirit, which is one Eternal God, to be judged according to their works, whether they be good or whether they be evil.

The doctrine of restoration is one of the central teachings of the Book of Mormon. It can bring hope and joy to people, such as the aging high priest, who sees the promise that he will at some future point have his missing hair, teeth, and virility restored; or it can be a source of fear and trembling for people, such as another aging high priest, who realizes that the questionable business practices he engaged in early in his career are now promising to bring him a bright recollection of all his guilt. "What goes around, comes around" is a pop culture phrase that captures the flavor of this doctrine, as does the more traditional Biblical injunction, "whatsoever a man soweth, that shall he also reap" (Galatians 6:7).

> Alma 13:30 — And may the Lord grant unto you repentance, that ye may not bring down his wrath upon you, that ye may not be bound down by the chains of hell, that ye may not suffer the second death.

When we read that Alma asked the Lord to grant his listeners repentance, we may be struck by the thought that many times we have prayed that the Lord would grant blessings to our families, friends, and leaders—maybe even once in a great while to our enemies. However, have we ever prayed that the Lord would grant anyone repentance?

After all, repentance is a great blessing. Thinking about it, I would like to believe that if I have done something wrong, others would pray for me that I might be blessed with repentance. Perhaps those prayers on my behalf would help to soften my heart and bring me to my knees in repentance.

When I am concerned about others, then, especially members of my family, perhaps I should pray that they will be granted repentance; that is, that they will be led to seek forgiveness in an attitude of humility. Of course, I should not pray for these things from an attitude of pride, but from an attitude of charity—an attitude I can have only if *I* am humble and repentant. Alma has set a wonderful example of just that kind of approach.

> Alma 17:2 — Now these sons of Mosiah were with Alma at the time the angel first appeared unto him; therefore Alma did rejoice exceedingly to see his brethren; and what added more to his joy, they were still his brethren in the Lord; yea, and they had waxed strong in the knowledge of the truth; for they were men of a sound understanding and they had searched the scriptures diligently, that they might know the word of God.
>
> 3 — But this is not all; they had given themselves to much prayer, and fasting; therefore they had the spirit of prophecy, and the spirit of revelation, and when they taught, they taught with power and authority of God.

The sons of Mosiah are Book of Mormon characters about whom many words have been written. I can even remember in the late 1960s seeing a rock band named "The Sons of Mosiah." They played one evening in Utah. Although not many LDS parents back in the sixties would have wanted their sons to run off and join a rock band, I'm sure they would have been pleased to have sons of whom it could be said, "They were men of a sound understanding and they had searched the scriptures diligently, that they might know the word of God." More than four decades later (can the sixties really be that far behind us?), most LDS parents would still be proud to have such words be said of their sons.

But, of course, there was more than scripture study that could be attributed to these young men. They prayed, they fasted, they had the spirit of prophecy and revelation, and thus when they taught, it was with the power and authority of God. The sons of Mosiah were quite the band of brothers!

The key point of these verses is that none of the characteristics that marked the sons of Mosiah are anything extraordinary. Scripture study, prayer, and fasting are not esoteric disciplines; they are basic, straightforward practices that can help anyone obtain the spirit of prophecy and revelation and teach the gospel with power and authority. We may never find ourselves mentioned in scripture or have rock bands named after us, but we can do the same things that the sons of Mosiah did and enjoy similar blessings. More important, we can be instruments in the Lord's hands to bless the lives of others as they did.

> Alma 17:25 — But Ammon said unto him: Nay, but I will be thy servant. Therefore Ammon became a servant to king Lamoni. And it came to pass that he was set among other servants to watch the flocks of Lamoni, according to the custom of the Lamanites.

How many of us would turn down these proffered gifts and reply, "But I will be thy servant"? This is quite a strategy! What is especially striking about this story is that it seems to capture the imaginations of those who read it, young and old alike. It somehow strikes us as truly bold and unusual—nearly unimaginable—for a young man such as Ammon to offer to be a mere servant.

But why does it seem so unusual? Paul, for example, often described himself as a servant of Christ. Earlier in the Book of Mormon, King Benjamin spoke of himself—and us—as servants. We should be familiar with the language and imagery of being a servant. Even the Lord himself spoke of being a servant.

Truth be told, however, many of us seem to have an easier time accepting the idea of servitude when we conceive of it as a noble metaphor—when we contemplate these scriptural discussions of servitude to which I just alluded. Accepting the idea of someone, such as Ammon, offering to become a literal servant of another person is quite different. Isn't it interesting—and telling—that we can read the scriptures and accept without much trouble the idea of someone being visited by an angel, but when we read of someone offering to be a servant to another, it strikes us as something highly unusual?

> Alma 18:36 — Now when Ammon had said these words, he began at the creation of the world, and also the creation of Adam, and told him all the things concerning the fall of man, and rehearsed and laid before him the records and the holy scriptures of the people, which had been spoken by the prophets, even down to the time that their father, Lehi, left Jerusalem.

This is a pattern we will encounter in several places in the Book of Mormon. A speaker or writer will begin with an account of the Creation and the Fall and then move on to the scriptures. Although the record does not say so here, my guess would be that Ammon's account of the scriptures would have shown his listeners how the scriptures point the way to the redemption of fallen mankind through the Atonement of Christ.

In our day, CES instructors have been counseled to teach students about what are sometimes called the "Three Pillars": Creation, Fall, and Atonement. Here we see Ammon teaching by that same pattern back in his day. It is a pattern by which we have often been taught throughout our lives in the gospel, and it is a pattern that we should remember and use when we teach our children and our students, and when we are blessed with missionary opportunities.

> Alma 22:3 — And now, O king, if thou wilt spare our lives, we will be thy servants. And the king said unto them: Arise, for I will grant unto you your lives, and I will not suffer that ye shall be my servants; but I will insist that ye shall administer unto me; for I have been somewhat troubled in mind because of the generosity and the greatness of the words of thy brother Ammon; and I desire to know the cause why he has not come up out of Middoni with thee.

The words "troubled in mind" seem to leap off the page to stimulate my imagination as I read this verse. Most of us have been troubled in mind at various times in our lives, and we all know of people who have been or are now troubled in mind.

For many people, being troubled in mind is what leads them to seek out and sometimes ultimately to accept the message of the gospel. In my own case, for example, I was quite troubled in mind during my sophomore year of high school. For reasons that I can no longer clearly recall, although I am sure they probably had something to do with a desire to be perceived as some sort of cool, ultra-intelligent intellectual, I had come to the decision that there was no God and therefore I was going to live my life as an atheist—a cool, ultra-intelligent atheist, no doubt.

Although I wanted to be an atheist, I did not want to be a hypocrite, so I felt duty-bound to stop attending church. My family had never been particularly religious, although my sisters and I had been baptized in the Methodist Church, which my family would attend in streaks. At the time I decided that I was going to be an atheist, we were in the middle of one of those streaks, so I knew that at some point I was going to have to summon up my courage and announce to my father that I no longer believed in God and thus no longer should be required to attend church.

It took some time to build up my courage, but finally I told him, late one night when just the two of us were sitting in the kitchen of our small house. Not surprisingly, he was dismayed at my announcement.

But then he said something that I found quite surprising. He asked me whether this meant I did not believe in Christ, either.

To be honest, I had not thought much about Christ, who was never really discussed in our home. Although I had recited creeds that outlined the Trinitarian concept of God, I had never thought about what they meant. At this point in my life, the whole idea of God and Christ and salvation seemed to be a great mystery that I no longer wanted to solve.

When my dad asked me about Christ, who to him was not an abstract concept but rather a real person, I was taken aback for a few moments. To suddenly start talking about Christ would complicate things and offer my dad a chance to put off making a decision about whether or not I could be excused from attending church. Because I wanted to keep the discussion with my dad as simple as possible, I quickly replied that no, I did not believe in Christ either.

When I said this, my father looked genuinely hurt, which surprised me even more. I thought my dad was asking me about Christ just to complicate the discussion. I had never imagined that he had any real commitment to Christ, but his face showed genuine pain when I said I did not believe in Jesus. After thinking things over for a short time, he told me that if I really did not want to attend church, he would not force me to do so.

I felt relieved and liberated at his surprising surrender. For a brief time, I enjoyed staying home on Sunday mornings. Soon, however, I found myself feeling more and more troubled in mind. Just when I thought I had decided my whole religious future by rejecting God, Christ, and church attendance in one fell swoop, I suddenly found myself more urgently troubled than ever about the whole issue of religion. Somehow, I knew my mind would not be settled until I found out the real truth about God. Even though I thought I had rejected the whole idea of God, I needed to ease my troubled mind. In such a condition, I was ready to accept the true gospel the moment I heard it, and that is what happened to me.

In thinking about the phrase "troubled in mind," I also think of the story of Joseph Smith, who was troubled in mind as a teenager. His troubled mind led him to the Sacred Grove, where he was ready to receive the true gospel.

When we are truly troubled in mind, we should earnestly seek the truth. Only the truth will be powerful enough to ease our mental and spiritual burden.

Note also in this verse that it was the "generosity and greatness of the words" of Ammon that caused the king to be troubled in mind. Perhaps we should sometimes pray not just that we might be good examples to others, but rather that our actions and our words might be strong enough to bring trouble to the minds of those with whom we associate so that they might be motivated to seek for truth and embrace it when they find it.

Finally, note that the most "troubling" characteristic of Ammon was his complete willingness to serve. If we pray for the opportunity to be good examples, we must be willing to humble ourselves and seek to serve, not merely to influence, those with whom we hope to share the gospel. We can perhaps best trouble them in mind by serving them in love.

> Alma 22:15 — And it came to pass that after Aaron had expounded these things unto him, the king said: What shall I do that I may have this eternal life of which thou hast spoken? Yea, what shall I do that I may be born of God, having this wicked spirit rooted out of my breast, and receive his Spirit, that I may be filled with joy, that I may not be cast off at the last day? Behold, said he, I will give up all that I possess, yea, I will forsake my kingdom, that I may receive this great joy.
>
> 16 — But Aaron said unto him: If thou desirest this thing, if thou wilt bow down before God, yea, if thou wilt repent of all thy sins, and will bow down before God, and call on his name in faith, believing that ye shall receive, then shalt thou receive the hope which thou desirest.

Having been troubled in mind to the point where he is ready to make a significant change in his life, the king expresses his desire to embrace the truth and his willingness to sacrifice his considerable wealth to obtain the great joy that the Spirit can bring. Had he been speaking with Nehor rather than Aaron, he would have been given the opportunity to turn his wealth over to the Nehorite church; from Aaron, however, the king learns that salvation is not for sale.

Instead, Aaron teaches the king a great pattern. From your desire, you can be moved to repent and call on God in faith, and then you will receive hope. Desire, repentance, faith, and hope—this is the pattern of the gospel, and those who pass through these stages are on their way to having charity, the true love of Christ, to restore their broken hearts.

> Alma 23:6 — And as sure as the Lord liveth, so sure as many as believed, or as many as were brought to the knowledge of the truth, through the preaching of Ammon and his brethren, according to the spirit of revelation and of prophecy, and the power of God working miracles in them—yea, I say unto you, as the Lord liveth, as many of the Lamanites as believed in their preaching, and were converted unto the Lord, never did fall away.

In this verse we are told the factors that contributed to the conversion of many Lamanites. They were brought to a knowledge of the truth by a combination of preaching, "the spirit of revelation and prophecy, and the power of God working miracles in them." As written, this verse seems ambiguous as to whom the word "them" refers—to those who came to believe, or to Ammon and his brethren. My suspicion is that the intent of the reference is more likely the latter than the former, but in either case, the words ring true. Surely the spirit of revelation and prophecy was manifest in both in those who received the word and those who delivered it, and surely the power of God worked miracles both in the Lamanites and in Ammon and his brethren.

It is the same for us today. When we attend a particularly powerful sacrament meeting or fireside, we can observe the workings of the Spirit and feel the miraculous power of the Lord at work both in the speaker and in those assembled. Surely, never is a speaker so filled with the Spirit as when those who have come to listen are also filled with the

Spirit. When this happens, miracles occur and the process of conversion is enhanced in the lives of those so touched.

> Alma 24:12 — Now, my best beloved brethren, since God hath taken away our stains, and our swords have become bright, then let us stain our swords no more with the blood of our brethren.
>
> 13 — Behold, I say unto you, Nay, let us retain our swords that they be not stained with the blood of our brethren; for perhaps, if we should stain our swords again they can no more be washed bright through the blood of the Son of our great God, which shall be shed for the atonement of our sins.
>
> 14 — And the great God has had mercy on us, and made these things known unto us that we might not perish; yea, and he has made these things known unto us beforehand, because he loveth our souls as well as he loveth our children; therefore, in his mercy he doth visit us by his angels, that the plan of salvation might be made known unto us as well as unto future generations.
>
> 15 — Oh, how merciful is our God! And now behold, since it has been as much as we could do to get our stains taken away from us, and our swords are made bright, let us hide them away that they may be kept bright, as a testimony to our God at the last day, or at the day that we shall be brought to stand before him to be judged, that we have not stained our swords in the blood of our brethren since he imparted his word unto us and has made us clean thereby.

The imagery in these verses is quite remarkable. Notice, for example, the brightness of the swords. We might be inclined to think of brightly polished swords, glinting in the sunlight, ready for battle; here, however, the brightness of the swords is said to show that they have not been stained by the blood of their victims—the brethren of the swordsmen.

In the next verse, the king goes on to remark that if their swords are stained by the blood of their brethren, then it may well be that "they can no more be washed bright through the blood of the Son of our great God." The blood of their brethren would stain the sword, but the blood of the Savior washes them bright. The contrasting images of the two bloods—the blood that stains and the blood that washes—are vivid and memorable.

The king next says how wonderful it is that the Lord has shown His mercy by revealing the plan of salvation. He exclaims in great joy, "Oh, how merciful is our God!" As we read these verses, we may find ourselves thinking about not only the mercy of our Lord, but also those things in our own lives that we have buried so they will no longer keep us from being clean. We should also note that the swords were hidden away only after they had been made clean. If we are to put our sins behind us (bury our swords), we must first repent (clean them). If we try to simply hide our sins or leave them behind without fully repenting, it is as though we have buried our bloodstained swords—the stains will be preserved and will come to haunt us. We must "bury our swords clean" by repenting, not by trying to hide them from others or the Lord.

> Alma 24:30 — And thus we can plainly discern, that after a people have been once enlightened by the Spirit of God, and have had great knowledge of things pertaining to righteousness, and then have fallen away into sin and transgression, they become more hardened, and thus their state becomes worse than though they had never known these things.

Whenever we encounter Book of Mormon phrases such as "and now we see," or as in this instance, "and thus we can plainly discern," we know that we are going to be presented with some sort of spiritual lesson. As we continue to read about how those who have been spiritually enlightened can actually be worse off after falling away than they would have been had they never been enlightened in the first place, we may well immediately think ahead to the ultimate tragic fate of the Nephites after they had fallen away. We can also liken this scripture unto ourselves by remembering how hard it is to turn back into the light after we have allowed ourselves to stray into darkness. Our shame and embarrassment make us more defensive, and we tend to harden ourselves against the loving entreaties of those who care about us most.

> Alma 25:15 — Yea, and they did keep the law of Moses; for it was expedient that they should keep the law of Moses as yet, for it was not all fulfilled. But notwithstanding the law of Moses, they did look forward to the coming of Christ, considering that the law of Moses was a type of his coming, and believing that they must keep those outward performances until the time that he should be revealed unto them.
>
> 16 — Now they did not suppose that salvation came by the law of Moses; but the law of Moses did serve to strengthen their faith in Christ; and thus they did retain a hope through faith, unto eternal salvation, relying upon the spirit of prophecy, which spake of those things to come.

Here we can feel the difference between the law of Moses, which is something we keep (affecting what we do), and faith in Christ, which is something we have within us (affecting who we are). At the same time, though, we also see how keeping the law of Moses helped the people have faith in Christ, and how their faith in Christ gave them hope for their eternal salvation. In these passages, the law of Moses and faith in Christ are portrayed not as two distinctly different kinds of things, as we sometimes characterize them, but rather as stages of a spiritual continuum.

We might also take a moment to observe that these people still looked forward in faith to the coming of Christ, which had not yet occurred. In our lives, there are ways in which our observance of law and ritual—temple ordinances, for example—serves to sustain our hope for eternal life and remind us that Christ will come again. In keeping the "law" of the temple, we point ourselves, with faith in Christ, toward eternal things that are promised us but not yet fully given to us.

> Alma 26:2 — And now, I ask, what great blessings has he bestowed upon us? Can ye tell?

And now we should ask ourselves, "What great blessings has He bestowed upon us?" Can we tell? Can we count them, and "name them one by one"? To contemplate our blessings is in itself a blessing. To testify of our blessings can be a blessing not only to us, but to others.

> Alma 26:3 — Behold, I answer for you; for our brethren, the Lamanites, were in darkness, yea, even in the darkest abyss, but behold, how many of them are brought to behold the marvelous light of God! And this is the blessing which hath been bestowed upon us, that we have been made instruments in the hands of God to bring about this great work.

Can we relate to this sentiment in our own experiences? Have we been blessed to be instruments in the hands of God to bring about a great work—or even a humble work? Do we pray to be a blessing as well as to be blessed?

> Alma 26:8 — Blessed be the name of our God; let us sing to his praise, yea, let us give thanks to his holy name, for he doth work righteousness forever.

Do we sing the praises of our God? Do we sing the songs of redeeming love in our sacrament meetings and family home evenings? Do our lives resonate with righteous rhythms and heavenly harmonies?

> Alma 26:11 — But Ammon said unto him: I do not boast in my own strength, nor in my own wisdom; but behold, my joy is full, yea, my heart is brim with joy, and I will rejoice in my God.

It is always stimulating to read these words of Ammon: "I do not boast in my own strength, nor in my own wisdom; but behold, my joy is full." Ammon shows such exuberance and joy, such deep-rooted enthusiasm for the gospel, that it is hard not to become excited about the gospel as we read his words.

There are times when we feel a quiet reverence for the Lord, as when we are in the temple, but there should be times when our feelings for the Lord and His temple should not be quiet and peaceful, but energetic and outgoing. We tend to associate the Lord and His temple with quiet moments of reverence and meditation, but we need to remember that our feelings for the Lord and His temple are also expressed in the mighty Hosanna Shout, wherein we simply can't contain our joy—our hearts are truly "brim with joy," and we rejoice out loud in our God.

The Lord wants us to not only have joy in His service, but also to be energized by that joy so that we can use that energy to expand our service and build up the kingdom. At times we do indeed need to boast—not in ourselves, but in our God. Ammon has shown us that we need not be reticent, that we really can let out some energy in the praise and service of the Lord.

> Alma 26:12 — Yea, I know that I am nothing; as to my strength I am weak; therefore I will not boast of myself, but I will boast of my God, for in his strength I can do all things; yea, behold, many mighty miracles we have wrought in this land, for which we will praise his name forever.

Does Ammon have a self-esteem problem? He says that he knows he is nothing and that he is weak. But rather than hold him back, his knowledge of his own inadequacies is what draws him to the Lord, the true source of strength. He speaks of the miracles in which he has participated; however, he does not do so to boast of his own accomplishments. Instead, he immediately expresses his gratitude to the Lord for making the miracles possible. And although Ammon does not explicitly say so, I'm sure that he recognizes the miracles that have been performed in his own soul as well as the miracles performed in public.

> Alma 26:16 — Therefore, let us glory, yea, we will glory in the Lord; yea, we will rejoice, for our joy is full; yea, we will praise our God forever. Behold, who can glory

> too much in the Lord? Yea, who can say too much of his great power, and of his mercy, and of his long-suffering towards the children of men? Behold, I say unto you, I cannot say the smallest part which I feel.

Can you feel the intense energy packed into this verse? Can you sense that Ammon is about to burst with spiritual power? Can you see and hear him speaking not in the measured tones of a General Authority at general conference, but with thunder in his voice and lightning in his eyes? Can you hear him speaking directly to you?

Can we—do we—glory too much in the Lord? Can we—do we—say too much of His power, mercy, and long-suffering? If we do say such powerful things, can we—do we—feel as though we have not yet begun to say the smallest part of what we feel? Can we—do we—feel the power of the Book of Mormon?

> Alma 26:17 — Who could have supposed that our God would have been so merciful as to have snatched us from our awful, sinful, and polluted state?

Who'd a-thunk it? Who indeed would really have supposed that God would be so merciful?

On one hand, we know that the scriptures testify of Christ and His great atoning sacrifice, but on the other hand, if there is anything with which we are completely and intimately familiar, it is our own sense of guilt and shame for the sins and weaknesses that continually drag us down.

It is heartbreaking to contemplate the misery of those individuals who have sufficient knowledge of Christ to believe that only He can save them, but who lack sufficient faith to believe that they themselves really can be forgiven. Sadly, there are those who believe that Christ can forgive sin, but who lack the faith to believe that *their* sins can be forgiven. There are those who readily profess that Christ has the power to create the world, overcome death, and order the limitless universe, yet these same people somehow feel their sins cannot be forgiven.

To think this way is in a subtle but real sense to deny the power of

Christ. Surely that is not the intent of these unhappy souls, but that is the undeniable implication of what they have come to believe.

Yes, as we ponder the mercy of Christ, it can be a shock to realize that our sins can be truly forgiven. Who would have supposed that our God would be so merciful? It hardly seems possible. It does not seem to be logical. It is an overwhelming thought, seemingly too grand to grasp with our mortal minds. We can only grasp it in our hearts, and at that, only if our hearts are broken.

Who indeed would have supposed such a thing? Such is the wonder and mystery of the gospel, so wonderfully expressed by Ammon in a remarkably straightforward way.

> Alma 26:21 — And now behold, my brethren, what natural man is there that knoweth these things? I say unto you, there is none that knoweth these things, save it be the penitent.

The simple but profound truths of the gospel of Christ can never be truly known by the heart or mind of the natural man. Only the penitent, those with humble minds and broken hearts, can hope to possess this saving knowledge.

> Alma 26:22 — Yea, he that repenteth and exerciseth faith, and bringeth forth good works, and prayeth continually without ceasing—unto such it is given to know the mysteries of God; yea, unto such it shall be given to reveal things which never have been revealed; yea, and it shall be given unto such to bring thousands of souls to repentance, even as it has been given unto us to bring these our brethren to repentance.

Ammon then goes on to explain more fully how we can come to have deep spiritual knowledge—through repentance, faith, service, and prayer—and how those who acquire such knowledge can serve to bring others to repentance, thus putting them too on the path to spiritual knowledge. This verse is a key verse to unlocking the secrets of how to obtain spiritual knowledge and perform successfully as a missionary.

> Alma 26:35 — Now have we not reason to rejoice? Yea, I say unto you, there never were men that had so great reason to rejoice as we, since the world began; yea, and my joy is carried away, even unto boasting in my God; for he has all power, all wisdom, and all understanding; he comprehendeth all things, and he is a merciful Being, even unto salvation, to those who will repent and believe on his name.
>
> 36 — Now if this is boasting, even so will I boast; for this is my life and my light, my joy and my salvation, and my redemption from everlasting wo. Yea, blessed is the name of my God, who has been mindful of this people, who are a branch of the tree of Israel, and has been lost from its body in a strange land; yea, I say, blessed be the name of my God, who has been mindful of us, wanderers in a strange land.
>
> 37 — Now my brethren, we see that God is mindful of every people, whatsoever land they may be in; yea, he numbereth his people, and his bowels of mercy are over all the earth. Now this is my joy, and my great thanksgiving; yea, and I will give thanks unto my God forever. Amen.

As he concludes his powerful discourse, Ammon returns to the question of boasting. He exults in the joy that the gospel brings and boasts of the power, wisdom, and mercy of God. As we read the phrase "lost from its body in a strange land," perhaps we can hear echoes of the story of Abraham, that wanderer in a strange land, or of Nephi's brother Jacob, who lamented the wanderings of his family as he so movingly closed his record. Perhaps we might reflect for a moment on how Abraham, Jacob, and Ammon were profoundly aware of the plight of their wandering peoples, but were also profoundly aware of the hope offered by the great and merciful plan of their God.

Given that we live in a telestial world, it is probably for the best that, from time to time, we do find ourselves feeling like wanderers in a strange land. After all, a telestial world should not feel like home to those who have a celestial birthright.

At those moments when we feel like wanderers in a strange land, we can take comfort in knowing that the path we should follow has been laid out before us. We are not strangers to the Holy One of Israel, who awaits us at the end of our journey. We may be wanderers in a strange land, but we can also be fellow citizens with the saints, citizens of Zion, and joint-heirs with Christ of all the Father hath.

With Ammon, then, we will feel joy and thanksgiving. We will feel motivated to thank the Lord for the knowledge we have obtained about our place in life, for we know that "God is mindful of every people, whatsoever land they may be in."

> Alma 27:16 — And it came to pass that as Ammon was going forth into the land, that he and his brethren met Alma, over in the place of which has been spoken; and behold, this was a joyful meeting.
>
> 17 — Now the joy of Ammon was so great even that he was full; yea, he was swallowed up in the joy of his God, even to the exhausting of his strength; and he fell again to the earth.
>
> 18 — Now was not this exceeding joy? Behold, this is joy which none receiveth save it be the truly penitent and humble seeker of happiness.

Having read Ammon's mighty sermon, we should not be surprised to read of the extreme joy he felt in being reunited with Alma. Note that this "exceeding joy" was not just because he had met Alma again, but also because he was "swallowed up in the joy of his God," such great joy being reserved for "the truly penitent and humble seeker of happiness."

Note further the words, "seeker of happiness." At first glance, this phrase might seem a bit out of place. After all, aren't we often admonished to forgo worldly pleasures and seek instead the Kingdom of God?

How wonderful it is that the Book of Mormon teaches us that humans really are sent to this earth with a divine commission to seek joy and that another name for the plan of salvation is the plan of happiness. To find this true spiritual happiness, we must be humble and penitent. We are not to seek mere temporal pleasure, but to humble ourselves to seek true joy and happiness. What can bring more joy and happiness than to know our sins have been forgiven and we are on the path that leads to eternal life? This is what it means to be a humble seeker of happiness.

> Alma 28:13 — And thus we see how great the inequality of man is because of sin and transgression, and the power of the devil, which comes by the cunning plans which he hath devised to ensnare the hearts of men.
>
> 14 — And thus we see the great call of diligence of men to labor in the vineyards of the Lord; and thus we see the great reason of sorrow, and also of rejoicing—sorrow because of death and destruction among men, and joy because of the light of Christ unto life.

Here we encounter another "and thus we see" passage. In this instance, the lesson that we are taught concerns the root cause of the great inequalities to be found among humankind, that root cause being sin and transgression, part of the cunning snares set by the devil.

From this observation, we then proceed immediately to another "and thus we see" passage, which explains that as a consequence of the sin and inequality that exists among humankind, the righteous are called to serve diligently. In addition, we are taught—and thus we see—that the world contains both great sorrow, with death and destruction all around us, and also great joy, with the light of Christ illuminating the way to life and salvation.

> Alma 29:1 — O that I were an angel, and could have the wish of mine heart, that I might go forth and speak with the trump of God, with a voice to shake the earth, and cry repentance unto every people!
>
> 2 — Yea, I would declare unto every soul, as with the voice of thunder, repentance and the plan of redemption, that they should repent and come unto our God, that there might not be more sorrow upon all the face of the earth.

> 3 — But behold, I am a man, and do sin in my wish; for I ought to be content with the things which the Lord hath allotted unto me.
>
> 4 — I ought not to harrow up in my desires, the firm decree of a just God, for I know that he granteth unto men according to their desire, whether it be unto death or unto life; yea, I know that he allotteth unto men, yea, decreeth unto them decrees which are unalterable, according to their wills, whether they be unto salvation or unto destruction.
>
> 5 — Yea, and I know that good and evil have come before all men; he that knoweth not good from evil is blameless; but he that knoweth good and evil, to him it is given according to his desires, whether he desireth good or evil, life or death, joy or remorse of conscience.
>
> 6 — Now, seeing that I know these things, why should I desire more than to perform the work to which I have been called?

Regardless of how many times we may have read these impassioned words of Alma, or had them quoted to us in sacrament meeting talks, firesides, and Sunday School classes, they never seem to lose their power to inspire us. If anything, they seem to gain power when we encounter them again and again.

This time through, I was struck by the comparisons and contrasts that I could draw between Alma's words and the plan presented by Satan in the premortal realm. Whereas Satan desired be like God, Alma is content to wish that he were an angel, albeit an angel with great powers. Whereas Satan vowed to save every soul, Alma desires to declare repentance and the plan of redemption to every soul. Whereas Satan wants all to be saved so that the glory would be his, Alma wanted all to repent and come unto God so that there might be no more sorrow. Whereas Satan fought hard to force his plan upon all, Alma realizes that he is in danger of going too far with his desires, and he concedes that God has granted agency to all so that they can choose life or death for themselves. Whereas Satan rebelled openly against God, Alma recognizes and respects the Lord's plan, and declares his desire to further the work of the Lord by humbly performing the work to which he has been called—to preach repentance and faith in Christ.

> Alma 29:9 — I know that which the Lord hath commanded me, and I glory in it. I do not glory of myself, but I glory in that which the Lord hath commanded me; yea, and this is my glory, that perhaps I may be an instrument in the hands of God to bring some soul to repentance; and this is my joy.
>
> 10 — And behold, when I see many of my brethren truly penitent, and coming to the Lord their God, then is my soul filled with joy; then do I remember what the Lord has done for me, yea, even that he hath heard my prayer; yea, then do I remember his merciful arm which he extended towards me.

Alma declares that he glories not in himself, but in what can be accomplished when he is an instrument in the hands of the Lord in bringing someone into repentance. Not only does he glory in it, he receives joy. Expanding on this theme, he says that when he sees not just one but many souls repenting and coming to the Lord, then he is filled with joy.

At this juncture, he then reveals something that is quite touching. He explains that when he sees others come unto Christ, it makes him recall what the Lord has done for him. Seeing the merciful arm of the Lord being extended to others reminds Alma of how the merciful arm of the Lord was extended to him. When we see others repent and experience the mighty change of heart, it can touch our souls today just as it touched the soul of Alma.

> Alma 30:13 — O ye that are bound down under a foolish and a vain hope, why do ye yoke yourselves with such foolish things? Why do ye look for a Christ? For no man can know of anything which is to come.

Even today we can find those who would chide the Saints for "yoking themselves with such foolish things." Moreover, there are many within the Church who have occasionally felt "yoked" by the responsibilities of home teaching, family home evening, ward council meetings, missionary service, and other obligations attendant to our membership. Still, if I am going to be yoked, then let me be yoked by Christ, who has promised that His yoke is easy and His burden light.

> Alma 30:16 — Ye look forward and say that ye see a remission of your sins. But behold, it is the effect of a frenzied mind; and this derangement of your minds comes because of the traditions of your fathers, which lead you away into a belief of things which are not so.

Frenzy and derangement of mind are not attributes we would typically associate with our belief in Christ and the Atonement. As we read these strong, almost violent words of Korihor, we can begin to sense that if anyone is possessed of a frenzied and deranged mind, it is he. We can also sense that such talk would begin to get under the skin of even the most patient believer, which makes the reaction of Alma seem to be a case of measured fury.

> Alma 30:33 — And notwithstanding the many labors which I have performed in the church, I have never received so much as even one senine for my labor; neither has any of my brethren, save it were in the judgment-seat; and then we have received only according to law for our time.
>
> 34 — And now, if we do not receive anything for our labors in the church, what doth it profit us to labor in the church save it were to declare the truth, that we may have rejoicings in the joy of our brethren?

I can hear in my mind the words "one senine" being uttered quite emphatically, perhaps even vehemently. In his next breath, however, it seems that Alma has already begun to curb his temper, and his charity returns when he refers to the joy of his brethren. As we read this verse, many of us will recall words of King Benjamin, who also spoke of his labors for his brethren and sisters.

In my own mind, I also think of the challenge put forward by my stake president, who has urged us to work toward becoming a "Zion stake," and who also sets an example for us by his tireless "labor in the church." When we liken the scriptures unto ourselves, it can also bring us joy to liken others unto the scriptures.

> Alma 30:43 — And now Korihor said unto Alma: If thou wilt show me a sign, that I may be convinced that there is a God, yea, show unto me that he hath power, and then will I be convinced of the truth of thy words.

Do you ever find yourself wishing or praying that the Lord would show you some kind of sign? There are times when the temptation to do so seems to be more than you can bear.

Such a time for me was when I was going to take the names of my parents and grandparents to the temple to do their temple work. Although I felt that I should not do so, I found myself wishing and ultimately praying, almost apologetically, for some kind of sign or manifestation that my parents were aware and pleased that their temple work was being performed. Although the Lord in His mercy did answer my prayer in a most unexpected way, I still had the feeling that I had asked for something it would have been better not to seek, and my prayers subsequent to that memorable temple trip were prayers of both gratitude and repentance.

Far happier and more grateful have been my prayers on those few but indelibly memorable occasions in my life when I have received a sign or spiritual confirmation completely unexpectedly. On those occasions, my joy was full and my gratitude was overflowing. Great is the mercy of the Lord!

> Alma 30:47 — But behold, it is better that thy soul should be lost than that thou shouldst be the means of bringing many souls down to destruction, by thy lying and by thy flattering words; therefore if thou shalt deny again, behold God shall smite thee, that thou shalt become dumb, that thou shalt never open thy mouth any more, that thou shalt not deceive this people any more.

The opening words of this verse bring to mind the story of Laban in the Book of Mormon. Although I have heard people question how the slaying of Laban could be justified, I have never heard anyone advocate strongly on behalf of Korihor. No, Korihor was not slain in the same manner as Laban, but the underlying principle is the same. The same principle, but on a far grander scale, underlies the Atonement: one soul suffers and is slain so that all might have the opportunity to escape spiritual destruction.

> Alma 31:5 — And now, as the preaching of the word had a great tendency to lead the people to do that which was just—yea, it had had more powerful effect upon the minds of the people than the sword, or anything else, which had happened unto them—therefore Alma thought it was expedient that they should try the virtue of the word of God.

This is another verse that we often hear from over the pulpit. It contains a powerful testimonial to the efficacy of the word of God. When I read this verse, I am reminded of another "verse" of contemporary scripture, President Boyd K. Packer's oft-quoted dictum that "true doctrine, understood, changes attitudes and behavior."[2] An aspect of this verse is sometimes overlooked. This statement about the power of the word is not presented simply as self-evident doctrine or armchair speculation, but is presented together with augmenting evidence: "Yea, it had had more powerful effect upon the minds of the people than the sword, or anything else that had happened to them." Note that second "had," which grounds this statement firmly in actual experience rather than mere opinion; in addition, note how the experience cited consists of much more than the effects of the sword.

Yes, the word of God is powerful, but when we add our experience and testimony to the word of God, our discourse has more power and we can achieve more in the service of the Lord than if we were merely to repeat what we have been taught. Alma speaks with great power not just because of his knowledge, but also because of his experience, which has tempered and refined his knowledge and enhanced his spiritual credibility.

Alma 31:12 — Now, when they had come into the land, behold, to their astonishment they found that the Zoramites had built synagogues, and that they did gather themselves together on one day of the week, which day they did call the day of the Lord; and they did worship after a manner which Alma and his brethren had never beheld;

13 — For they had a place built up in the center of their synagogue, a place for standing, which was high above the head; and the top thereof would only admit one person.

14 — Therefore, whosoever desired to worship must go forth and stand upon the top thereof, and stretch forth his hands towards heaven, and cry with a loud voice, saying:

15 — Holy, holy God; we believe that thou art God, and we believe that thou art holy, and that thou wast a spirit, and that thou art a spirit, and that thou wilt be a spirit forever.

16 — Holy God, we believe that thou hast separated us from our brethren; and we do not believe in the tradition of our brethren, which was handed down to them by the childishness of their fathers; but we believe that thou hast elected us to be thy holy children; and also thou hast made it known unto us that there shall be no Christ.

17 — But thou art the same yesterday, today, and forever; and thou hast elected us that we shall be saved, whilst all around us are elected to be cast by thy wrath down to hell; for the which holiness, O God, we thank thee; and we also thank thee that thou hast elected us, that we may not be led away after the foolish traditions of our brethren, which doth bind them down to a belief of Christ, which doth lead their hearts to wander far from thee, our God.

18 — And again we thank thee, O God, that we are a chosen and a holy people. Amen.

> 19 — Now it came to pass that after Alma and his brethren and his sons had heard these prayers, they were astonished beyond all measure.
>
> 20 — For behold, every man did go forth and offer up these same prayers.
>
> 21 — Now the place was called by them Rameumptom, which, being interpreted, is the holy stand.
>
> 22 — Now, from this stand they did offer up, every man, the selfsame prayer unto God, thanking their God that they were chosen of him, and that he did not lead them away after the tradition of their brethren, and that their hearts were not stolen away to believe in things to come, which they knew nothing about.
>
> 23 — Now, after the people had all offered up thanks after this manner, they returned to their homes, never speaking of their God again until they had assembled themselves together again to the holy stand, to offer up thanks after their manner.

Like Alma, when I read the account of the Zoramites and their ritual prayers upon the Rameumptom, I find myself "astonished beyond all measure." The account reads almost like a literary parody of an apostate people. At times, in fact, I have wondered whether this account of the Zoramite mode of worship was based on actual eyewitness observation or was instead based on an ancient American form of urban legend. But when I think of the strange things that can happen among those who have been misled by religious charlatans, and when I think of the strange teachings that may have been circulated by false teachers such as Nehor, Korihor, and the corrupt priests of King Noah, I am willing to accept that the Zoramite form of worship may well have been every bit as astonishing as here portrayed.

The Rameumptom is another of the striking and memorable images from the Book of Mormon. Indeed, that strange word is part of the vocabulary of the Latter-day Saints. At this very moment, somebody somewhere is very likely teasing somebody else about getting up on his Rameumptom. To do so is a common LDS rhetorical ploy, something that makes us a peculiar people indeed. Viva la Rameumptom!

> Alma 31:35 — Behold, O Lord, their souls are precious, and many of them are our brethren; therefore, give unto us, O Lord, power and wisdom that we may bring these, our brethren, again unto thee.

Although Alma was astonished by the worship practices of the Zoramites, he does not abandon the Zoramites to go look for a more receptive audience. Instead, he exemplifies charity by pleading with the Lord in their behalf, culminating in his tender declaration that "their souls are precious."

It is easy for us to think of our children and grandchildren as having precious souls, or our most dear friends, but what about those of other faiths, especially those of other faiths who may have said hard, hurtful things about our faith and our people? Can we honestly say that we think their souls are precious? To do so, we must have charity, which we can only develop through repentance, faith, and service, as Alma did.

> Alma 32:1 — And it came to pass that they did go forth, and began to preach the word of God unto the people, entering into their synagogues, and into their houses; yea, and even they did preach the word in their streets.
>
> 2 — And it came to pass that after much labor among them, they began to have success among the poor class of people; for behold, they were cast out of the synagogues because of the coarseness of their apparel—

These verses—save for the King James style of language—read as though they could have been written about our full-time missionaries today, who preach the word to the people in their churches, their homes, and out in the streets. After a lot of hard work and a lot of rejections, they begin to have some success among the poor. This coming Sunday, many LDS missionaries around the world will report in their missionary correlation meetings that they have begun teaching some people who are facing considerable temporal challenges, but who are receptive to the gospel. It seems as though the humble of circumstance are more likely to respond to the message of the missionaries, just like in the time of Alma.

> Alma 32:14 — And now, as I said unto you, that because ye were compelled to be humble ye were blessed, do ye not suppose that they are more blessed who truly humble themselves because of the word?
>
> 15 — Yea, he that truly humbleth himself, and repenteth of his sins, and endureth to the end, the same shall be blessed—yea, much more blessed than they who are compelled to be humble because of their exceeding poverty.
>
> 16 — Therefore, blessed are they who humble themselves without being compelled to be humble; or rather, in other words, blessed is he that believeth in the word of God, and is baptized without stubbornness of heart, yea, without being brought to know the word, or even compelled to know, before they will believe.

Alma speaks of those who are compelled to be humble, in this case because of poverty. He says that they are blessed, but invites them to think of those who are humbled not by external circumstances, but because of their faith in the word of God. He adds a beatitude in verse 16: "blessed are they who humble themselves without being compelled to be humble," which means that those who accept the word of God willingly—without having to be painstakingly persuaded or in some extreme instances, compelled to accept it—are deeply blessed.

Perhaps it would be good to reflect upon this teaching by considering a particular case. For example, consider the case of a man who pays his tithing, but does so grudgingly, primarily because of the pressure he feels from his wife and his bishop. Yes, he is paying his tithing, and he will surely be blessed for it more so than if he did not pay it; however, he would no doubt find himself more deeply blessed were he to humbly accept and embrace the principle of tithing and pay it willingly. If nothing else, he would be blessed by having a happier heart and less troubled mind. It might also mean he would be blessed by having a better relationship with his wife, being more rewardingly engaged in his priesthood duties, and enjoying his life more fully. He truly would be more blessed by paying his tithing humbly and willingly than if he paid his tithing because he had been compelled to do so.

We could cite our own instances where we have seen that humble acceptance and compliance with the word of God has brought blessings in our lives that we could not have received had we complied only grudgingly because of real or perceived outside pressure. When we choose freely to humble ourselves and seek to do the will of the Lord, our hearts become more open to the profound joy that only the Spirit can impart to us.

Alma has offered us a valuable insight into how we may bring more and better joy into our lives. Can we accept it without having to be compelled to do so?

> Alma 32:26 — Now, as I said concerning faith—that it was not a perfect knowledge—even so it is with my words. Ye cannot know of their surety at first, unto perfection, any more than faith is a perfect knowledge.

Having previously asserted that it is best to accept the word of God without having to be compelled to do so, Alma then goes on to offer some practical advice about how this can be achieved. It is fascinating how Alma recognizes that even if he is preaching the true word of God, what he says is not self-evident, so we cannot be expected to accept his words at face value. At the same time, he knows that it will not be well for us if we are somehow compelled to accept his words, so he must offer us a way that we can humbly accept for ourselves what he has to say, and by extension, accept for ourselves the word of God.

> Alma 32:27 — But behold, if ye will awake and arouse your faculties, even to an experiment upon my words, and exercise a particle of faith, yea, even if ye can no more than desire to believe, let this desire work in you, even until ye

> believe in a manner that ye can give place for a portion of my words.

Alma goes on to propose his famous experiment, which is familiar to us both from our own readings of this chapter and from the countless lessons and talks that have been delivered on the theme of Alma's experiment upon the word. For many of us, the experiment is itself a word that we have taken into our hearts and felt grow into something that has yielded fruit in our own lives. Because we have experimented upon the experiment upon the word, we now know for ourselves that what Alma taught us is true.

> Alma 32:41 — But if ye will nourish the word, yea, nourish the tree as it beginneth to grow, by your faith with great diligence, and with patience, looking forward to the fruit thereof, it shall take root; and behold it shall be a tree springing up unto everlasting life.
>
> 42 — And because of your diligence and your faith and your patience with the word in nourishing it, that it may take root in you, behold, by and by ye shall pluck the fruit thereof, which is most precious, which is sweet above all that is sweet, and which is white above all that is white, yea, and pure above all that is pure; and ye shall feast upon this fruit even until ye are filled, that ye hunger not, neither shall ye thirst.
>
> 43 — Then, my brethren, ye shall reap the rewards of your faith, and your diligence, and patience, and long-suffering, waiting for the tree to bring forth fruit unto you.

As we in our own lives have experimented upon the words of Alma's experiment upon the word, we have been rewarded by coming to an understanding of how we can learn gospel principles. Through our faith, patience, and diligence in experimenting upon the word, we not only feel the word grow within us, but we also grow ourselves as we are feast on the precious fruit, which is not only sweet, but also nourishing and life-enhancing.

Alma makes a point throughout his teachings of stressing the importance of growing faith through time and experience. Although he is primarily remembered for his zeal ("Oh, that I were an angel"), his true character as revealed through his teachings seems to be that of a spiritual pragmatist, a teacher who emphasizes diligence, patience, and long-suffering in dealing with the challenges of life. In Lehi's vision of the tree of life, the fruit was already there, waiting to be plucked and enjoyed; in Alma's metaphor, we must wait for the tree to bring forth fruit. We must patiently nurture our faith, but if we do, we are rewarded as the fruit of our faith comes forth to nurture us.

Alma counsels us to experiment upon the word with patience, promising us that if we do so, we will be bountifully and beautifully rewarded. President Hinckley made a similar promise in urging us to read the Book of Mormon. As we read the Book of Mormon in response to his challenge, we are indeed experimenting upon his words, nurturing the fruit that he promised us if we would follow his counsel.

> Alma 33:11 — And thou didst hear me because of mine afflictions and my sincerity; and it is because of thy Son that thou hast been thus merciful unto me, therefore I will cry unto thee in all mine afflictions, for in thee is my joy; for thou hast turned thy judgments away from me, because of thy Son.

Here is another of those verses that I had never really noticed before in my previous readings of the Book of Mormon, but which now strikes me as a precious little jewel. "Thou didst hear me because of mine afflictions and my sincerity" is a phrase that captures the essence of true repentance. As we become aware of our sins, they do become afflictions to us; as we humble ourselves to truly seek forgiveness from the Lord, we become sincere. The Lord then hears us because of our afflictions and our sincerity. What a beautiful thought!

But not only is this verse beautiful in an aesthetic sense, it also expresses profound doctrinal truth, particularly about the nature of

Christ and the Atonement: "it is because of thy Son that thou has been thus merciful unto me . . . for thou hast turned thy judgments away from me, because of thy Son."

Another striking phrase from this verse is "therefore I will cry unto thee in all mine afflictions, for in thee is my joy." The contrast between the affliction that Zenos finds in himself and the joy he will find in the Lord illustrates quite vividly the beauty and blessing of true repentance.

It is a shame that we have only a few verses from the prophet Zenos in our scriptures, for he was obviously a man of profound spiritual and poetic gifts. We should be thankful that Alma has given us this tantalizing excerpt from Zenos, for even in this small snippet there is much to ponder and enjoy.

Alma then gives us an excerpt from another nearly unknown prophet, Zenock, which also contains much to ponder and enjoy:

> Alma 33:12 — And now Alma said unto them: Do ye believe those scriptures which have been written by them of old?
>
> 13 — Behold, if ye do, ye must believe what Zenos said; for, behold he said: Thou hast turned away thy judgments because of thy Son.
>
> 14 — Now behold, my brethren, I would ask if ye have read the scriptures? If ye have, how can ye disbelieve on the Son of God?
>
> 15 — For it is not written that Zenos alone spake of these things, but Zenock also spake of these things—
>
> 16 — For behold, he said: Thou art angry, O Lord, with this people, because . . .

Because what? Why would the Lord be angry with these people of whom Zenock speaks? A good friend of mine who is a CES Director likes to throw this question out to his Institute students, who typically offer examples of various sins the people may have committed, such as turning to idolatry, not keeping the Sabbath, committing adultery, and other such transgressions of the Law of Moses.

How about us? How would we complete this verse? I would imagine that most of us would offer transgressions similar to those offered by the students. Indeed, unless we are already familiar with this verse, we may be surprised to read the rest of the verse and discover that the Lord is angry with these people not because they have transgressed the Law of Moses, but because

> 16 — . . . they will not understand thy mercies which thou hast bestowed upon them because of thy Son.

When we take stock of our own spiritual condition, do we ever think to ask ourselves whether we understand and are grateful for the mercies that have been bestowed upon us? When we thank the Lord for our blessings, do we think primarily of our temporal blessings? Do we ever reflect upon the tender mercies that have been freely given to us through the Atonement of the Savior? By quoting Zenock to us, Alma has given us much food for thought.

> Alma 33:23 — And now, my brethren, I desire that ye shall plant this word in your hearts, and as it beginneth to swell even so nourish it by your faith. And behold, it will become a tree, springing up in you unto everlasting life. And then may God grant unto you that your burdens may be light, through the joy of his Son. And even all this can ye do if ye will. Amen.

In the wake of his discourse on the experiment, Alma closes his remarks by asking his listeners to actually experiment upon the words he has just given them. Once again we see a reference to the tree as a symbol of eternal life. Alma employs this powerful metaphor, which has made many appearances in the written record of the Nephites and which was no doubt a rhetorical theme passed down through generations of Nephite priesthood leaders.

> Alma 34:9 — For it is expedient that an atonement should be made; for according to the great plan of the Eternal God there must be an atonement made, or else all mankind must unavoidably perish; yea, all are hardened; yea, all are fallen and are lost, and must perish except it

> be through the atonement which it is expedient should be made.
>
> 10 — For it is expedient that there should be a great and last sacrifice; yea, not a sacrifice of man, neither of beast, neither of any manner of fowl; for it shall not be a human sacrifice; but it must be an infinite and eternal sacrifice.

When a person gives up his or her life in behalf of a cause or a nation, we honor that as the ultimate sacrifice, something that we can scarcely imagine. Still, that is only a finite human sacrifice. Had Jesus of Nazareth died on the cross as a man, the son of Joseph, that too would have been only a finite human sacrifice. Yes, it would have been what we would call today an ultimate sacrifice, but it would have been insufficient to atone for our sins and overcome the effects of the Fall.

But the crucifixion of Jesus was the sacrifice of the Christ, the son of the living God. It was an infinite and eternal sacrifice, sufficient to save and to justify. These two brief verses offer a succinct introduction to the Atonement, which is further explicated in the verses that follow.

> Alma 34:14 — And behold, this is the whole meaning of the law, every whit pointing to that great and last sacrifice; and that great and last sacrifice will be the Son of God, yea, infinite and eternal.
>
> 15 — And thus he shall bring salvation to all those who shall believe on his name; this being the intent of this last sacrifice, to bring about the bowels of mercy, which overpowereth justice, and bringeth about means unto men that they may have faith unto repentance.
>
> 16 — And thus mercy can satisfy the demands of justice, and encircles them in the arms of safety, while he that exercises no faith unto repentance is exposed to the whole law of the demands of justice; therefore only unto him that has faith unto repentance is brought about the great and eternal plan of redemption.

Here are more verses rich in doctrinal meaning, verses containing principles that we need to liken unto ourselves. As many times as I have read or heard discussed the phrase "this being the intent of this last sacrifice, to bring about the bowels of mercy, which overpowereth justice, and bringeth about means unto men that they may have faith unto repentance," it still strikes me each time with wonder and joy to think that mercy really will overpower justice, meaning that sin—even my sin—truly can be forgiven through the atoning power of Jesus Christ.

The phrase that immediately follows is also one we should take heed: "And bringeth about means unto men that they may have faith unto repentance." Mercy will overpower justice, which is certainly a felicitous miracle; however, mercy can only be applied in our lives through repentance. The Lord in His grace has made mercy available to us through repentance, but we must choose to repent and exercise faith. We must choose for ourselves life over death. Verse 16 makes this clear: "Therefore only unto him that has faith unto repentance is brought about the great and eternal plan of redemption."

As we contemplate these verses and seek to liken them unto ourselves, let us remember once again that when we joined the church, we were baptized unto repentance. What a wonderful blessing this is!

> Alma 34:17 — Therefore may God grant unto you, my brethren, that ye may begin to exercise your faith unto repentance, that ye begin to call upon his holy name, that he would have mercy upon you;
>
> 18 — Yea, cry unto him for mercy; for he is mighty to save.
>
> 19 — Yea, humble yourselves, and continue in prayer unto him.
>
> 20 — Cry unto him when ye are in your fields, yea, over all your flocks.
>
> 21 — Cry unto him in your houses, yea, over all your household, both morning, mid-day, and evening.
>
> 22 — Yea, cry unto him against the power of your enemies.

> 23 — Yea, cry unto him against the devil, who is an enemy to all righteousness.
>
> 24 — Cry unto him over the crops of your fields, that ye may prosper in them.
>
> 25 — Cry over the flocks of your fields, that they may increase.
>
> 26 — But this is not all; ye must pour out your souls in your closets, and your secret places, and in your wilderness.
>
> 27 — Yea, and when you do not cry unto the Lord, let your hearts be full, drawn out in prayer unto him continually for your welfare, and also for the welfare of those who are around you.

In these verses, we are reminded of the power and necessity of prayer and the need to pray not only for our own welfare, but also for the welfare of others. In the very next verse . . .

> Alma 34:28 — And now behold, my beloved brethren, I say unto you, do not suppose that this is all; for after ye have done all these things, if ye turn away the needy, and the naked, and visit not the sick and afflicted, and impart of your substance, if ye have, to those who stand in need— I say unto you, if ye do not any of these things, behold, your prayer is vain, and availeth you nothing, and ye are as hypocrites who do deny the faith.

. . . we are reminded of the necessity for action. Without action, our prayers may well be in vain. As the old maxim goes, we should "get on our knees and pray as though everything depends on God, then get up on our feet and work as though everything depends on us."

> Alma 34:32 — For behold, this life is the time for men to prepare to meet God; yea, behold the day of this life is the day for men to perform their labors.

This verse has great nostalgic value for me. When I first began attending Church meetings as an investigator back in the mid-sixties, Alma 34:32 was the MIA theme, which we would stand and recite each Wednesday evening as part of our opening exercises. I can still recall reciting those words in great solemnity.

In contrast to that solemnity, I must confess that when I encounter this verse now, the image that immediately pops into my mind is Elmer Fudd pointing his shotgun at Bugs Bunny and saying, "Say your pwayers, wabbit!" Somehow, though, I don't really think that kind of scenario is what Amulek had in mind when he spoke of preparing to meet God. Rather, he goes on to explain that repentance should not be procrastinated. Once the shotgun is pointed at you, it may be too late. Bugs Bunny always managed to survive, but we mere mortals might not be so fortunate.

Seriously speaking, we should not look at preparing to meet God simply in the sense that we could be taken at any time. We should also look at it in a positive sense: how blessed it is to live a godly life. As we exercise faith, repent in humility, seek the Lord in prayer, strive to keep our covenants, and labor diligently to serve others, we really are preparing ourselves to meet God by inviting His Spirit to be with us.

> Alma 36:17 — And it came to pass that as I was thus racked with torment, while I was harrowed up by the memory of my many sins, behold, I remembered also to have heard my father prophesy unto the people concerning the coming of one Jesus Christ, a Son of God, to atone for the sins of the world.
>
> 18 — Now, as my mind caught hold upon this thought, I cried within my heart: O Jesus, thou Son of God, have mercy on me, who am in the gall of bitterness, and am encircled about by the everlasting chains of death.
>
> 19 — And now, behold, when I thought this, I could remember my pains no more; yea, I was harrowed up by the memory of my sins no more.

Alma's account of his conversion is one of the most dramatic stories in the Book of Mormon. Generally, we see it as an example of the power of Christ to save and to bring about the mighty change of heart. We might also come to reflect on how the conversion of Alma, who had persecuted the Church but became such a great missionary, echoes the conversion of Paul, who also went from persecutor to missionary through the process of a miraculous conversion.

However, there is another, more subtle message we can glean from reflecting on Alma's account. As we read the phrase "while I was harrowed up by the memory of my many sins, behold, I remembered also to have heard my father prophesy unto the people concerning the coming of one Jesus Christ, a Son of God, to atone for the sins of the world," we might recall that Alma is in fact addressing these words to his son, Helaman. Alma is trying to pass along something of utmost importance to his son, in hopes that Helaman will realize the importance of having faith in Christ.

In our own lives, it is important that we too pass along our crucial knowledge to our own children and loved ones. We need to pass along our own stories of conversion, so our children and loved ones will have that extra witness of Christ that we can provide them to supplement and make more personal that which they may have heard from their teachers or read for themselves in the scriptures. Our personal testimonies of Christ may be the most influential factors in bringing our children and loved ones to their own change of heart, so we owe it to them to let our own testimonies be heard at the appropriate moments as revealed by the Spirit.

> Alma 37:6 — Now ye may suppose that this is foolishness in me; but behold I say unto you, that by small and simple things are great things brought to pass; and small means in many instances doth confound the wise.

To read of small and simple things bringing great things to pass gives us hope, for we often see our own lives as small and simple when compared to the grand scheme of things. Furthermore, as we look back over our lives, we can see that many of the things that were important factors in our lives were in themselves small and simple things. Prayer, although large in importance, is really a small and simple thing. The sacrament bread and water of which we partake each Sunday are in themselves small and simple things. Our wedding bands are small and simple things. These things and others, though similarly small and simple, have made profound differences in our lives. Our testimonies, which may be small and simple in their wording, may make all the difference in our lives and in the lives of those to whom we bear witness.

> Alma 37:33 — Preach unto them repentance, and faith on the Lord Jesus Christ; teach them to humble themselves and to be meek and lowly in heart; teach them to withstand every temptation of the devil, with their faith on the Lord Jesus Christ.
>
> 34 — Teach them to never be weary of good works, but to be meek and lowly in heart; for such shall find rest to their souls.
>
> 35 — O, remember, my son, and learn wisdom in thy youth; yea, learn in thy youth to keep the commandments of God.
>
> 36 — Yea, and cry unto God for all thy support; yea, let all thy doings be unto the Lord, and whithersoever thou goest let it be in the Lord; yea, let all thy thoughts be directed unto the Lord; yea, let the affections of thy heart be placed upon the Lord forever.
>
> 37 — Counsel with the Lord in all thy doings, and he will direct thee for good; yea, when thou liest down at night lie down unto the Lord, that he may watch over you in your sleep; and when thou risest in the morning let thy heart be full of thanks unto God; and if ye do these things, ye shall be lifted up at the last day.

What wonderful advice this is from a father to a son—and to us! Let us do as Alma counsels, lying down at night and rising each morning communing with the Lord, so that when we lie down for that last time, we may be ready to rise on that glorious morning with all restored in its fulness. To pray at night and to pray in the morning is a small and simple thing, but to be lifted up at the last day will be an incredibly great and glorious thing.

> 44 — For behold, it is as easy to give heed to the word of Christ, which will point to you a straight course to eternal bliss, as it was for our fathers to give heed to this compass, which would point unto them a straight course to the promised land.
>
> 45 — And now I say, is there not a type in this thing? For just as surely as this director did bring our fathers, by following its course, to the promised land, shall the words of Christ, if we follow their course, carry us beyond this vale of sorrow into a far better land of promise.

Alma draws a comparison between his fathers looking to the Liahona to be led to the promised land and his son looking to Christ to be led to a "far better land of promise," or in other words, eternal life. Alma wants his son to see that if he remains faithful, the way will be pointed before him. With our modern means of communication through which we can hear the words of the prophets twenty-four hours per day and our present-day situation of having temples within a relatively short distance from our doors, the way is certainly laid out before us if we will but have the faith to listen and obey. We would do well to heed Alma's advice.

But given the many advantages we have in our day, we would also do well to heed Alma's final warning and advice to his son:

> 46 — O my son, do not let us be slothful because of the easiness of the way; for so was it with our fathers; for so was it prepared for them, that if they would look they might live; even so it is with us. The way is prepared, and if we will look we may live forever.
>
> 47 — And now, my son, see that ye take care of these sacred things, yea, see that ye look to God and live. Go unto this people and declare the word, and be sober. My son, farewell.

We do need to be careful that we do not let the very "easiness of the way" cause us to slacken our stride. Often in our lives, there is a temptation to take things for granted. The very closeness of the temple, for example, may make going there seem less important. Knowing that we can turn on the television or the computer to gain instant access to the scriptures and words of the General Authorities may lull us into complacency—just knowing that the words are there whenever we need to see them may, paradoxically, mean that we actually look at them less.

In verse 47, I also note that Alma points his son both inward—to take care of these sacred things, which I read as both the actual physical objects with which he has been entrusted and the sacred teachings to which he has been exposed—and outward, to reach out to the people to declare the word. Here is another echo of the two great commandments, to love God and to love our neighbor. Here is more wonderful advice from a father to a son that we can read as a shadow and type of advice from a Heavenly Father to His children—to us.

> Alma 40:22 — Yea, this bringeth about the restoration of those things of which has been spoken by the mouths of the prophets.
>
> 23 — The soul shall be restored to the body, and the body to the soul; yea, and every limb and joint shall be restored to its body; yea, even a hair of the head shall not be lost; but all things shall be restored to their proper and perfect frame.

Once again we encounter the doctrine of restoration. Here, though, the focus is on the promise of actual physical restoration. These particular verses bring comfort to aging high priests, who can visualize someday having restored a head of hair, ears that can actually hear, eyes that can see, a nose that can smell, a mouthful of teeth, a back that no longer aches, a heart that needs no pacemaker, and hips and knees that no longer ache and creak.

> Alma 41:2 — I say unto thee, my son, that the plan of restoration is requisite with the justice of God; for it is

> requisite that all things should be restored to their proper order. Behold, it is requisite and just, according to the power and resurrection of Christ, that the soul of man should be restored to its body, and that every part of the body should be restored to itself.

Here, restoration is tied to justice. To the aging high priests, though, it seems tied more to mercy . . .

> Alma 41:4 — And if their works are evil they shall be restored unto them for evil. Therefore, all things shall be restored to their proper order, every thing to its natural frame—mortality raised to immortality, corruption to incorruption—raised to endless happiness to inherit the kingdom of God, or to endless misery to inherit the kingdom of the devil, the one on one hand, the other on the other—

The doctrine of restoration is discussed in several places in the Book of Mormon, but to see the doctrine of restoration from another perspective, it is instructive to take a look at section 76 of the Doctrine and Covenants. In the great vision of the eternal kingdoms, we see that men and women will end up in a kingdom that corresponds to the kind of life they lived here on the earth. Broadly speaking, section 76 indicates that those who love a lie and are not trustworthy are slated for the telestial kingdom, those who are of sound moral character but are not valiant in their testimony of the Savior are slated for the terrestrial kingdom, and those who are valiant and keep their covenants will inherit the celestial kingdom.

The sense we get from a reading of section 76 that men and women are destined for the kingdom that corresponds to the kind of life they lived here during mortality corresponds well to the sense we get of the doctrine of restoration as taught in the Book of Mormon. In section 76, more detail is given and more doctrines are added, but the basic doctrine of restoration is clearly implied, even though that term is not explicitly used. Here is an instance where our study of the Book of Mormon can assist us in gaining a deeper and more grounded understanding of the doctrines of the restoration.

> Alma 41:10 — Do not suppose, because it has been spoken concerning restoration, that ye shall be restored from sin to happiness. Behold, I say unto you, wickedness never was happiness.

"Wickedness never was happiness" is another of those phrases from the Book of Mormon that we hear over and over again in our meetings. It is also a favorite phrase for LDS parents to recite to their teenagers. Looking at it in its original context, we see that it refers not only to this life, but also to the life to come. There are wicked people who seem to be pretty happy, much to our chagrin, especially if we are trying to teach our teenagers, who are experts at finding counterexamples to any general principles we try to teach them. However, those who live wickedly are not going to find true happiness in the life to come. They are not going to be transformed in the twinkling of an eye.

Our teenagers need to be taught the full import of this verse: that what we sow, we shall reap. What we make of ourselves will be what we are, and what we will be. The Lord can work miracles in us, and we can experience the mighty change of heart, but only if we are humble and repentant, not proud and rebellious. If we want to be really happy, then we must follow the Lord, who can change us. If we do not follow the Lord, we will not attain a full measure of happiness.

No, wickedness never was happiness. Reflecting back on Mosiah 3:19, we might recall that "the natural man is an enemy to God, and has been from the fall of Adam, and will be, forever and ever, unless he yields to the enticings of the Holy Spirit, and putteth off the natural man and becometh a saint through the atonement of Christ the Lord." These are the kinds of things that our teenagers need to hear and understand. These are the things that the Book of Mormon teaches. This is why our teenagers need to read the Book of Mormon—and their parents and grandparents, too.

> Alma 41:14 — Therefore, my son, see that you are merciful unto your brethren; deal justly, judge righteously, and do good continually; and if ye do all these

> things then shall ye receive your reward; yea, ye shall have mercy restored unto you again; ye shall have justice restored unto you again; ye shall have a righteous judgment restored unto you again; and ye shall have good rewarded unto you again.
>
> 15 — For that which ye do send out shall return unto you again, and be restored; therefore, the word restoration more fully condemneth the sinner, and justifieth him not at all.

These two verses contain some really practical spiritual advice about how we should live. They also serve to further expand our understanding of the doctrine of restoration. Restoration does not apply only to what we are, physically and spiritually, it also applies to what we do. According to the popular phrase, "What goes around comes around." Restoration is something like that. What we do will be restored to us. As we saw in section 76, if we live a lie in this life, we will live amongst liars in the next life. But if we live faithfully and valiantly according to our testimony of the Savior, we will continue to do the Savior's will in the eternities.

As Alma points out to his son, this implication of the doctrine of restoration more fully reveals the consequences of sin and transgression. If we live a life that consists of doing things that separate us from God, without repenting, then we will in fact succeed in separating ourselves from God. The responsibility will be ours, for we are the agents of our actions.

> Alma 42:4 — And thus we see, that there was a time granted unto man to repent, yea, a probationary time, a time to repent and serve God.

Here is a clear and concise answer to that age-old question, "What is the purpose of life?" The purpose of life is to repent and serve God. The great blessing of life is that God grants most of us time to do so. Most of us need it.

> Alma 42:24 — For behold, justice exerciseth all his demands, and also mercy claimeth all which is her own;

> and thus, none but the truly penitent are saved.

And if someone follows up by asking, "What is so important about repentance?" here is another clear and concise answer: "None but the truly penitent are saved."

What had Nehor taught? He preached that all would be saved. But Alma clearly understands what was wrong with this false doctrine and wants to make sure that his son understands, too. This is a doctrine that we must teach our own children.

> Alma 42:29 — And now, my son, I desire that ye should let these things trouble you no more, and only let your sins trouble you, with that trouble which shall bring you down unto repentance.

Here is some more practical spiritual advice from a father to a son that we can apply in our own lives. We should not get obsessed with our weaknesses, failings, and sins, which are an inevitable part of our probationary state. We should let these things trouble us no more except to the extent that they lead us to repentance—that unto which we were baptized, let us remember once again.

As we reflect on Alma's advice, perhaps we will also reflect on what can be seen as the dual nature of sin. On one hand, sin is what estranges us from God. When we know we have sinned, we may even seek to hide from God. But if we train ourselves to deal with our sins as Alma suggests, then the knowledge of our sin can also function to draw us back to God as we seek Him in sincere repentance. Our very knowledge of our own propensity to sin can help to keep us humble, and if we are humble, we are better able to draw close to the Lord.

> Alma 46:8 — Thus we see how quick the children of men do forget the Lord their God, yea, how quick to do iniquity, and to be led away by the evil one.
>
> 9 — Yea, and we also see the great wickedness one very wicked man can cause to take place among the children of men.

Once again we encounter a spiritual lesson prefaced by "thus we see." We are reminded how quickly we can be estranged from God and goodness, which is something that if we are reflective about our spiritual condition, we will recognize as a real danger within our own lives.

As we think of truly evil people, we are also reminded how much evil one person can bring about. We might be tempted to reflect only on figures such as Laban, King Noah, Zeezrom, Hitler, Pol Pot, Mao, and perhaps others now living. However, we should also take a moment to think about ourselves. If we are led away, which we know can certainly happen, we really could bring about great evil, both for ourselves and for our loved ones. The bad example that we set could lead others to follow us down that slippery slope and thus multiply the misery.

We need to recognize that this possibility for wickedness lies within each of us. At the same time, though, we must remember Alma's counsel to let this trouble us only to the extent that it leads us to repentance. Let us be humbled by our recognition of our own weakness, but not humiliated.

> Alma 46:12 — And it came to pass that he rent his coat; and he took a piece thereof, and wrote upon it—In memory of our God, our religion, and freedom, and our peace, our wives, and our children—and he fastened it upon the end of a pole.

Moroni rending his coat to create the Title of Liberty is one of the striking images from the Book of Mormon, one that captures the imagination of young and old alike. It is worth pondering not just the drama of the story, but also the message that he wrote, particularly the order of that which he cited as important enough to fight for. First comes God Himself, then religion, and then freedom, which we can take to mean religious freedom in addition to political freedom. Next comes peace, which might be seen as an outgrowth of religious and political freedom. Note that as one who follows God and who understands the doctrines of salvation, Moroni cites principles, not things—religion, freedom, and peace. Then he cites people, but not politicians or generals, but rather families—their wives and their children.

Note also the things that Moroni does not cite their gold and silver, their cities, their government, their leaders, their prosperity, their lands, or their crops. Moroni is a man of high ideals; moreover, he is quite focused. He has a clear idea of what is really important and he is willing to fight for those things if he must.

> Alma 48:11 — And Moroni was a strong and a mighty man; he was a man of a perfect understanding; yea, a man that did not delight in bloodshed; a man whose soul did joy in the liberty and the freedom of his country, and his brethren from bondage and slavery;
>
> 12 — Yea, a man whose heart did swell with thanksgiving to his God, for the many privileges and blessings which he bestowed upon his people; a man who did labor exceedingly for the welfare and safety of his people.
>
> 13 — Yea, and he was a man who was firm in the faith of Christ, and he had sworn with an oath to defend his people, his rights, and his country, and his religion, even to the loss of his blood.

As many times as I have read the Book of Mormon, I always feel inspired when I read this account of the characteristics of Moroni. I want to believe that there are leaders like this today.

When we read verse 13, we would do well to liken this scripture to ourselves by thinking of the covenants we have taken upon ourselves at baptism and in the temple. Perhaps we will feel inspired by this account of the virtues of Moroni to the point that we will gain a renewed desire to live according to those covenants. We may not have the understanding, bravery, or strength of Moroni, but we can still live according to our covenants. Surely the Lord expects at least that of us.

> Alma 48:16 — And also, that God would make it known unto them whither they should go to defend themselves against their enemies, and by so doing, the Lord would deliver them; and this was the faith of

> Moroni, and his heart did glory in it; not in the shedding of blood but in doing good, in preserving his people, yea, in keeping the commandments of God, yea, and resisting iniquity.
>
> 17 — Yea, verily, verily I say unto you, if all men had been, and were, and ever would be, like unto Moroni, behold, the very powers of hell would have been shaken forever; yea, the devil would never have power over the hearts of the children of men.

Could this be said of you? If you were to substitute your name for Moroni's, would this verse still ring true? If you are faithfully living your covenants, then indeed it would.

> Alma 49:26 — And it came to pass that he was exceedingly angry with his people, because he had not obtained his desire over the Nephites; he had not subjected them to the yoke of bondage.
>
> 27 — Yea, he was exceedingly wroth, and he did curse God, and also Moroni, swearing with an oath that he would drink his blood; and this because Moroni had kept the commandments of God in preparing for the safety of his people.
>
> 28 — And it came to pass, that on the other hand, the people of Nephi did thank the Lord their God, because of his matchless power in delivering them from the hands of their enemies.

This passage offers quite a contrast between Amalickiah and Moroni. Amalickiah is angry with his people because he has not yet obtained his desire to enslave the Nephites. Moroni joins his people in thanking God for their deliverance, which was largely bought about by Moroni's courage and dedication. Amalickiah swears vengeance and says he will drink Moroni's blood, while Moroni keeps the commandments and relies upon the blood of the Lamb.

> Alma 51:4 — Therefore, those who were desirous that the law should be altered were angry with him, and desired

> that he should no longer be chief judge over the land; therefore there arose a warm dispute concerning the matter, but not unto bloodshed.

"A warm dispute . . . but not unto bloodshed" is a fascinating phrase. Do we have these sorts of disputes today? I believe we encounter accounts of them all the time, and we may well be embroiled in several of them ourselves, in our professions, our hobbies, or sometimes even within the walls of our own homes. If we can keep them from degenerating into bloodshed, the world will be a better place. Too many of our headline stories are accounts of warm disputes that got hot and escalated into bloodshed.

> Alma 53:20 — And they were all young men, and they were exceedingly valiant for courage, and also for strength and activity; but behold, this was not all—they were men who were true at all times in whatsoever thing they were entrusted.
>
> 21 — Yea, they were men of truth and soberness, for they had been taught to keep the commandments of God and to walk uprightly before him.

The description of the stripling warriors is another scripture we would love to liken unto ourselves. To be courageous, vigorous, trustworthy, and righteous is a noble goal. Perhaps it is best to begin by aiming to keep the commandments—and to be repentant. If we can do this, we can be more like the stripling warriors. We may never be as courageous or as strong and active (remember, these were "all young men," after all), but we can be as trustworthy, true, and sober. Remember, we too have been "taught to keep the commandments of God and to walk uprightly before him." In that respect, the stripling warriors have nothing on us.

> Alma 56:47 — Now they never had fought, yet they did not fear death; and they did think more upon the liberty of their fathers than they did upon their lives; yea, they had been taught by their mothers, that if they did not doubt, God would deliver them.

> 48 — And they rehearsed unto me the words of their mothers, saying: We do not doubt our mothers knew it.

We often recite that the stripling warriors were taught well by their mothers, but do we remember what they were taught? They had been taught that if they did not doubt—or, in other words, if they had faith—God would deliver them. It is clear from these verses that they had faith in their mothers, and from this faith they drew the strength to have faith in the Lord. We—mothers and fathers alike—must teach our children likewise. Perhaps even more important, we must live our lives in such a way that our children will have sufficient faith in us to pay heed to what we teach them about having faith in Christ.

> Alma 57:27 — Now this was the faith of these of whom I have spoken; they are young, and their minds are firm, and they do put their trust in God continually.

When I teach the Book of Mormon, I like to invite my students to liken this verse to themselves. I am confident that all of us would do well to do the same. Not all of us are young, but do we have firm minds, and put our trust in God continually? How do we measure up?

> Alma 60:23 — Do ye suppose that God will look upon you as guiltless while ye sit still and behold these things? Behold I say unto you, Nay. Now I would that ye should remember that God has said that the inward vessel shall be cleansed first, and then shall the outer vessel be cleansed also.

Here is another striking image from the Book of Mormon—cleaning first the "inward vessel" before cleaning the "outer vessel." We do not want to be hypocrites, nor do we want to do the right things for the wrong reasons. As it says in Proverbs, "For as he thinketh in his heart, so is he." This verse also invites comparison with the words of the Savior as recorded in Matthew:

> Matthew 23:25 — Woe unto you, scribes and Pharisees, hypocrites! for ye make clean the outside of the cup and of the platter, but within they are full of extortion and excess.
>
> 26 — Thou blind Pharisee, cleanse first that which is within the cup and platter, that the outside of them may be clean also.

As we liken these scriptures unto ourselves, we realize that we cannot hide from the Lord. If our inward vessel is not clean, we must repent, not pretend.

> Alma 60:36 — Behold, I am Moroni, your chief captain. I seek not for power, but to pull it down. I seek not for honor of the world, but for the glory of my God, and the freedom and welfare of my country. And thus I close mine epistle.

Here is yet another memorable phrase from the Book of Mormon: "I seek not for power, but to pull it down." This may be one of the hardest scriptures to liken to ourselves, for whether we are ready to admit it or not, there are significant ways in which we all seek for power. We often seek advantage in our relationships, even our loving relationships, because that would give us more power. We often want more power in our careers. We sometimes tend to seek more power within our families. Although we may be loathe to admit it, there are even those of us who have sought power in our church callings and assignments.

Even if we can honestly say with Captain Moroni that we seek not for power, but to pull it down, are we sure that our motive for pulling down power is not so we can thus have more power of our own? We must be so careful in this!

The lust for power is such a tricky thing—seductive and destructive. But power itself is a necessary thing, something that we must have to progress in life. As we reflect on the words of Captain Moroni, let us also reflect on that great latter-day discourse on power from the Doctrine and Covenants:

> D&C 121:41 — No power or influence can or ought to be maintained by virtue of the priesthood, only by persuasion, by long-suffering, by gentleness and meekness, and by love unfeigned;
>
> 42 — By kindness, and pure knowledge, which shall greatly enlarge the soul without hypocrisy, and without guile—
>
> 43 — Reproving betimes with sharpness, when moved upon by the Holy Ghost; and then showing forth afterwards an increase of love toward him whom thou hast reproved, lest he esteem thee to be his enemy;
>
> 44 — That he may know that thy faithfulness is stronger than the cords of death.
>
> 45 — Let thy bowels also be full of charity towards all men, and to the household of faith, and let virtue garnish thy thoughts unceasingly; then shall thy confidence wax strong in the presence of God; and the doctrine of the priesthood shall distil upon thy soul as the dews from heaven.
>
> 46 — The Holy Ghost shall be thy constant companion, and thy scepter an unchanging scepter of righteousness and truth; and thy dominion shall be an everlasting dominion, and without compulsory means it shall flow unto thee forever and ever.

If we seek for power, or to pull it down, we must do so in faithfulness. If we exercise power, we must do so with charity.

Notes

1. Bruce R. McConkie, "The Purifying Power of Gethsemane," *Ensign,* Apr. 1985, 9.
2. Boyd K. Packer, "Little Children," *Ensign,* Nov. 1986, 16.

Chapter 7

Helaman

I have always found that reaching the book of Helaman seems to be a significant milestone in reading the Book of Mormon, at least psychologically. For one thing, having read the Book of Mormon before, I know that the coming of the Savior is not too far off. Furthermore, the first time I ever read the Book of Mormon, I found chapter 12 of Helaman to be quite special; since then, I have always looked forward to reading it again so I can relive the excitement I felt as a teenager.

> Helaman 2:8 — And when the servant of Helaman had known all the heart of Kishkumen, and how that it was his object to murder, and also that it was the object of all those who belonged to his band to murder, and to rob, and to gain power, (and this was their secret plan, and their combination) the servant of Helaman said unto Kishkumen: Let us go forth unto the judgment-seat.

Hugh Nibley calls the "secret plan" the Master Mahan Principle—that is, one can murder to get gain. In contemplating this principle, we can see that it is the evil opposite of the Atonement. In the Atonement, one life is freely and lovingly given that all might gain. In the secret plan, life is cruelly taken so others might gain. In this same light, we can think of the Savior telling the rich young man that he should give away all he owns so that he might gain eternal life, then think of

Satan's plan as revealed to Cain—commit murder (thereby forsaking eternal life) to gain possessions.

> Helaman 3:25 — And so great was the prosperity of the church, and so many the blessings which were poured out upon the people, that even the high priests and the teachers were themselves astonished beyond measure.
>
> 26 — And it came to pass that the work of the Lord did prosper unto the baptizing and uniting to the church of God, many souls, yea, even tens of thousands.
>
> 27 — Thus we may see that the Lord is merciful unto all who will, in the sincerity of their hearts, call upon his holy name.
>
> 28 — Yea, thus we see that the gate of heaven is open unto all, even to those who will believe on the name of Jesus Christ, who is the Son of God.
>
> 29 — Yea, we see that whosoever will may lay hold upon the word of God, which is quick and powerful, which shall divide asunder all the cunning and the snares and the wiles of the devil, and lead the man of Christ in a strait and narrow course across that everlasting gulf of misery which is prepared to engulf the wicked—
>
> 30 — And land their souls, yea, their immortal souls, at the right hand of God in the kingdom of heaven, to sit down with Abraham, and Isaac, and with Jacob, and with all our holy fathers, to go no more out.

This passage bubbles over with spiritual joy, offering us many things to contemplate. For example, think for a moment about the idea that "so great was the prosperity of the church, and so many the blessings which were poured out upon the people, that even the high priests and the teachers were themselves astonished beyond measure." That might seem a bit far-fetched, but speaking as someone who is both a high priest and a teacher, I can honestly say that when I contemplate the prosperity of the church that enabled President Hinckley to dedicate so many temples in such a short span of time, and when I think of all the blessings that were poured out upon the people as a result of having these temples in our midst, I truly am astonished beyond measure. This is a verse we can relish likening to ourselves.

Another phrase that stands out—and notice that it is prefaced by "Yea, we see that"—is "whosoever will may lay hold upon the word of God." As we have been taught previously, if we have a desire to plant the word in our hearts, the word will bear fruit. What a powerful promise is made in verses 29 and 30! The gate is indeed open to all.

> Helaman 5:6 — Behold, my sons, I desire that ye should remember to keep the commandments of God; and I would that ye should declare unto the people these words. Behold, I have given unto you the names of our first parents who came out of the land of Jerusalem; and this I have done that when you remember your names ye may remember them; and when ye remember them ye may remember their works; and when ye remember their works ye may know how that it is said, and also written, that they were good.
>
> 7 — Therefore, my sons, I would that ye should do that which is good, that it may be said of you, and also written, even as it has been said and written of them.
>
> 8 — And now my sons, behold I have somewhat more to desire of you, which desire is, that ye may not do these things that ye may boast, but that ye may do these things to lay up for yourselves a treasure in heaven, yea, which is eternal, and which fadeth not away; yea, that ye may have that precious gift of eternal life, which we have reason to suppose hath been given to our fathers.
>
> 9 — O remember, remember, my sons, the words which king Benjamin spake unto his people; yea, remember that there is no other way nor means whereby man can be saved, only through the atoning blood of Jesus Christ, who shall come; yea, remember that he cometh to redeem the world.

Once again we find an example in the Book of Mormon of advice from a father to his sons—in this instance, the advice of Helaman to his sons—that offers valuable counsel for us today. Certainly we would be well advised to remember the words and the works of Lehi, Nephi and Jacob, to do that which is good, and to remember the words of King Benjamin. Were we to do so, then it is indeed likely that we will be remembered as good people.

> Helaman 5:12 — And now, my sons, remember, remember that it is upon the rock of our Redeemer, who is Christ, the Son of God, that ye must build your foundation; that when the devil shall send forth his mighty winds, yea, his shafts in the whirlwind, yea, when all his hail and his mighty storm shall beat upon you, it shall have no power over you to drag you down to the gulf of misery and endless wo, because of the rock upon which ye are built, which is a sure foundation, a foundation whereon if men build they cannot fall.

One of the most enduring images in scripture is "the rock." Simon Peter was known as the rock. Jesus himself is the chief cornerstone, hewn from rock. Here, we read of that bedrock upon which we must build if we are to endure the storms and stress that life and the devil will surely hurl our way.

Many of us surely remember rock singer Bob Seger singing about a pickup truck that was said to be tough and dependable "like a rock." Filmed in slow motion, that was one formidable truck, but out on the road, it seemed pretty ordinary. Let us hope our lives are not like that. When we look at our lives in "slow motion," perfectly framed, as when we are sitting in sacrament meeting on a Sunday morning, they might look pretty solid—but how did our lives look when we were out on the road on Saturday night? Let us hope that in our everyday lives, day in and night out, we truly are "like a rock."

> Helaman 7:10 — And behold, now it came to pass that it was upon a tower, which was in the garden of Nephi, which was by the highway which led to the chief market, which was in the city of Zarahemla; therefore, Nephi had bowed himself upon the tower which was in his garden,

which tower was also near unto the garden gate by which led the highway.

11 — And it came to pass that there were certain men passing by and saw Nephi as he was pouring out his soul unto God upon the tower; and they ran and told the people what they had seen, and the people came together in multitudes that they might know the cause of so great mourning for the wickedness of the people.

12 — And now, when Nephi arose he beheld the multitudes of people who had gathered together.

13 — And it came to pass that he opened his mouth and said unto them: Behold, why have ye gathered yourselves together? That I may tell you of your iniquities?

14 — Yea, because I have got upon my tower that I might pour out my soul unto my God, because of the exceeding sorrow of my heart, which is because of your iniquities!

15 — And because of my mourning and lamentation ye have gathered yourselves together, and do marvel; yea, and ye have great need to marvel; yea, ye ought to marvel because ye are given away that the devil has got so great hold upon your hearts.

16 — Yea, how could you have given way to the enticing of him who is seeking to hurl away your souls down to everlasting misery and endless wo?

17 — O repent ye, repent ye! Why will ye die? Turn ye, turn ye unto the Lord your God. Why has he forsaken you?

18 — It is because you have hardened your hearts; yea, ye will not hearken unto the voice of the good shepherd; yea, ye have provoked him to anger against you.

19 — And behold, instead of gathering you, except ye will repent, behold, he shall scatter you forth that ye shall become meat for dogs and wild beasts.

20 — O, how could you have forgotten your God in the very day that he has delivered you?

21 — But behold, it is to get gain, to be praised of

men, yea, and that ye might get gold and silver. And ye have set your hearts upon the riches and the vain things of this world, for the which ye do murder, and plunder, and steal, and bear false witness against your neighbor, and do all manner of iniquity.

22 — And for this cause wo shall come unto you except ye shall repent. For if ye will not repent, behold, this great city, and also all those great cities which are round about, which are in the land of our possession, shall be taken away that ye shall have no place in them; for behold, the Lord will not grant unto you strength, as he has hitherto done, to withstand against your enemies.

23 — For behold, thus saith the Lord: I will not show unto the wicked of my strength, to one more than the other, save it be unto those who repent of their sins, and hearken unto my words. Now therefore, I would that ye should behold, my brethren, that it shall be better for the Lamanites than for you except ye shall repent.

24 — For behold, they are more righteous than you, for they have not sinned against that great knowledge which ye have received; therefore the Lord will be merciful unto them; yea, he will lengthen out their days and increase their seed, even when thou shalt be utterly destroyed except thou shalt repent.

25 — Yea, wo be unto you because of that great abomination which has come among you; and ye have united yourselves unto it, yea, to that secret band which was established by Gadianton!

26 — Yea, wo shall come unto you because of that pride which ye have suffered to enter your hearts, which has lifted you up beyond that which is good because of your exceedingly great riches!

27 — Yea, wo be unto you because of your wickedness and abominations!

28 — And except ye repent ye shall perish; yea, even your lands shall be taken from you, and ye shall be destroyed from off the face of the earth.

> 29 — Behold now, I do not say that these things shall be, of myself, because it is not of myself that I know these things; but behold, I know that these things are true because the Lord God has made them known unto me, therefore I testify that they shall be.

When I read the account of Nephi's sermon from the tower, with its depiction of the prophet praying in a conspicuous place, with a crowd gathering around to see what he is up to, only to realize that he is in fact lamenting their wickedness out loud to the Lord, I cannot help but imagine that Nephi had a voice something like actor/director Mel Brooks, especially when I read the line, "Behold, why have ye gathered yourselves together? That I may tell you of your iniquities?" Imagine the cutting tone that Mel Brooks's voice could have brought to that line! Although the subject is a serious one, I cannot read this verse and keep a straight face. I keep picturing this whole scene as though it were an outtake from Brooks's movie *History of the World, Part One,* complete with a fake beard on the actor playing Nephi.

I hope I have not permanently ruined these passages for you, as there is much here of great value. What we might especially want to take from this account is the realization that even though Nephi comes close to expressing contempt for those who have gathered to hear him, he still preaches repentance. He still offers them the chance to exercise their agency and come unto Christ. His language may be pointed, but his message is still one of invitation. He speaks with sharpness, but with the inspiration of the Spirit.

What is especially striking is how Nephi balances his message of the Lord's anger with his message of the Lord's mercy. He reminds them that the Lord has forsaken them because they have forsaken the Lord—but if they will repent, the Lord will spare them.

> Helaman 10:4 — Blessed art thou, Nephi, for those things which thou hast done; for I have beheld how thou hast with unwearyingness declared the word, which I have given unto thee, unto this people. And thou hast not feared them, and hast not sought thine own life, but hast sought

my will, and to keep my commandments.

5 — And now, because thou hast done this with such unwearyingness, behold, I will bless thee forever; and I will make thee mighty in word and in deed, in faith and in works; yea, even that all things shall be done unto thee according to thy word, for thou shalt not ask that which is contrary to my will.

6 — Behold, thou art Nephi, and I am God. Behold, I declare it unto thee in the presence of mine angels, that ye shall have power over this people, and shall smite the earth with famine, and with pestilence, and destruction, according to the wickedness of this people.

7 — Behold, I give unto you power, that whatsoever ye shall seal on earth shall be sealed in heaven; and whatsoever ye shall loose on earth shall be loosed in heaven; and thus shall ye have power among this people.

8 — And thus, if ye shall say unto this temple it shall be rent in twain, it shall be done.

9 — And if ye shall say unto this mountain, Be thou cast down and become smooth, it shall be done.

10 — And behold, if ye shall say that God shall smite this people, it shall come to pass.

11 — And now behold, I command you, that ye shall go and declare unto this people, that thus saith the Lord God, who is the Almighty: Except ye repent ye shall be smitten, even unto destruction.

Here is a scripture that we might especially desire to liken unto ourselves, for all of us would love to have the Lord declare that we are blessed because of the things that we have done. As much as we might love to imagine such a thing, we would have a hard time imagining that we have captured the Lord's attention because of our unwearying devotion to spreading His word. We remember all too vividly the home teaching that we did not quite get around to last month, or the shut-in we had planned to visit but something came up, or the friend at school we have been meaning to give a copy of the Book of Mormon to but have never quite seemed to find the right moment.

Still, we can imagine what it would be like to have the powers that the Lord promises Nephi: that whatever we say, the Lord will bring about. As we think about what it would be like to have such great power bestowed upon us, we should also pay careful heed to what the Lord says about Nephi, that Nephi "shalt not ask that which is contrary to my will." Perhaps that is the part of this scripture that we ought to liken unto ourselves.

Indeed, although it is unlikely that any of us will have a revelation where the Lord will promise us such great powers, each of us can attempt to live in such a way that we do not seek for ourselves or for others that which is contrary to God's will. As we reflect further upon this passage of scripture, we might also come to realize that we have been promised great powers in our patriarchal and other priesthood blessings, and that these powers have been promised to us contingent upon our faith and worthiness—or, in other words, contingent upon our submitting ourselves to the will of the Lord.

Nephi understood the will of the Lord and submitted to it. And what was the will of the Lord? Did the Lord want Nephi to flatten mountains or to call fire from heaven down upon the people? No, the Lord wanted the people to repent. The Lord wanted Nephi to preach repentance.

That is the great lesson found in these verses, a lesson we can liken unto ourselves. We need to seek the will of the Lord and to do the work of the Lord, realizing that the work of the Lord is to bring to pass the immortality and eternal life of man and that only the repentant will inherit eternal life. That is why we, like Nephi, must preach and teach repentance to our families and friends and even our enemies. That is why we, like Nephi, have been blessed with power from the Lord.

> Helaman 12:4 — O how foolish, and how vain, and how evil, and devilish, and how quick to do iniquity, and how slow to do good, are the children of men; yea, how quick to hearken unto the words of the evil one, and to set their hearts upon the vain things of the world!
>
> 5 — Yea, how quick to be lifted up in pride; yea, how

quick to boast, and do all manner of that which is iniquity; and how slow are they to remember the Lord their God, and to give ear unto his counsels, yea, how slow to walk in wisdom's paths!

6 — Behold, they do not desire that the Lord their God, who hath created them, should rule and reign over them; notwithstanding his great goodness and his mercy towards them, they do set at naught his counsels, and they will not that he should be their guide.

7 — O how great is the nothingness of the children of men; yea, even they are less than the dust of the earth.

8 — For behold, the dust of the earth moveth hither and thither, to the dividing asunder, at the command of our great and everlasting God.

As we read these verses and sense the passion with which they were written, we to may be led to lament how wicked and foolish human beings can be. We may well begin to wonder how it is that the Lord still cares for us at all. What a vivid portrait of human vanity these verses paint! We can hardly be blamed if we feel discouraged after reading them, even if we are lifted by the eloquence and power of the language.

Helaman 12:23 — Therefore, blessed are they who will repent and hearken unto the voice of the Lord their God; for these are they that shall be saved.

24 — And may God grant, in his great fulness, that men might be brought unto repentance and good works, that they might be restored unto grace for grace, according to their works.

But after all the discouragement we feel as we contemplate human frailty, still there is hope to be found in the goodness and mercy of our God. As foolish, vain, and ungrateful as we men and women may be, the Lord loves us. He will hear our prayers of repentance and acknowledge our humble obedience to His commandments. We are not forgotten, we are not forsaken. We have hope in Christ.

> Helaman 13:22 — Ye do not remember the Lord your God in the things with which he hath blessed you, but ye do always remember your riches, not to thank the Lord your God for them; yea, your hearts are not drawn out unto the Lord, but they do swell with great pride, unto boasting, and unto great swelling, envyings, strifes, malice, persecutions, and murders, and all manner of iniquities.

Samuel cuts close to the bone here, speaking in great plainness. Do we today have some of the same problems? Do we forget the things with which the Lord has blessed us and dwell instead on our own prosperity? If we are prosperous, do we count it as a blessing, or simply as a confirmation of our own cleverness—an affirmation of our ambition? Are we in danger of sliding downward from pride and boasting into envy and iniquity?

It is crucial for us to show gratitude for our blessings. It is not that God wants and needs to be thanked, it is rather that we need to be thankful. Nor is it just that we need to recognize our blessings, it is also that we need to recognize our need to share our blessings with others.

> Helaman 13:25 — And now when ye talk, ye say: If our days had been in the days of our fathers of old, we would not have slain the prophets; we would not have stoned them, and cast them out.
>
> 26 — Behold ye are worse than they; for as the Lord liveth, if a prophet come among you and declareth unto you the word of the Lord, which testifieth of your sins and iniquities, ye are angry with him, and cast him out and seek all manner of ways to destroy him; yea, you will say that he is a false prophet, and that he is a sinner, and of the devil, because he testifieth that your deeds are evil.

Ouch! Once again, Samuel cuts close to the bone. The typical reading that we would do out loud in a Sunday School setting—hesitant, polite, restrained—would not begin to capture the cutting quality that must have been in Samuel's voice as he delivered these words.

And surely there was plenty of gesturing and gesticulating going on—Samuel is on a roll!

> Helaman 13:38 — But behold, your days of probation are past; ye have procrastinated the day of your salvation until it is everlastingly too late, and your destruction is made sure; yea, for ye have sought all the days of your lives for that which ye could not obtain; and ye have sought for happiness in doing iniquity, which thing is contrary to the nature of that righteousness which is in our great and Eternal Head.
>
> 39 — O ye people of the land, that ye would hear my words! And I pray that the anger of the Lord be turned away from you, and that ye would repent and be saved.

As cutting as Samuel's accusations are, though, he still offers hope. With as much passion as he has poured out in condemnation of his audience, he is willing to pray for their salvation. The contrast between these two verses is remarkable.

Are we able to do this in our own lives? Are we willing to pray for those we criticize and condemn? Can we honestly say that we hate the sin but love the sinner?

> Helaman 14:30 — And now remember, remember, my brethren, that whosoever perisheth, perisheth unto himself; and whosoever doeth iniquity, doeth it unto himself; for behold, ye are free; ye are permitted to act for yourselves; for behold, God hath given unto you a knowledge and he hath made you free.
>
> 31 — He hath given unto you that ye might know good from evil, and he hath given unto you that ye might choose life or death; and ye can do good and be restored unto that which is good, or have that which is good restored unto you; or ye can do evil, and have that which is evil restored unto you.

And what if the sinner is us? Are we willing to pray for our own salvation? Or will we just remain in a state of self-pity, too critical of ourselves to feel good about our lives but too proud of ourselves to truly seek help?

There is plenty in these verses to "remember, remember." If we perish, we perish unto ourselves. We have been given the great blessings of knowledge and agency, so we cannot perish through ignorance or through coercion.

If we choose to follow the Lord, then He is with us. We are saved with our families and our dead to whom we have been sealed, and we are fellow citizens with the saints. We are not alone on the strait and narrow path.

Chapter 8

3 Nephi through 4 Nephi

When we finish the book of Helaman, we know that the Savior will be coming soon. No matter how many times we have read the Book of Mormon, we still get a heightened sense of anticipation. We dread the destruction that we know will be visiting these people, but at the same time we look forward to the joy that will be felt by the faithful who survive the destruction and live to see the coming of the Lord.

If we stop to examine these feelings, we begin to see that perhaps we are experiencing a finite peek into the infinite. As we feel both dread and joy at the destruction and glory to come, we may sense in some small finite way what the Lord experienced in His infinite knowledge and wisdom. He knew then far better than we know now what was to come for these people, many of whom would soon experience terror and others of whom would experience ecstasy from His mighty arm.

If we do reflect on the Lord in this way, we may also begin to appreciate how careful, thoughtful, and persistent scripture study can bring us closer to the Lord. As we liken the word of the Lord unto ourselves, in some measure we are also likening the Lord unto ourselves.

> 3 Nephi 1:10 — Now it came to pass that when Nephi, the son of Nephi, saw this wickedness of his people, his heart was exceedingly sorrowful.

> 11 — And it came to pass that he went out and bowed himself down upon the earth, and cried mightily to his God in behalf of his people, yea, those who were about to be destroyed because of their faith in the tradition of their fathers.
>
> 12 — And it came to pass that he cried mightily unto the Lord all that day; and behold, the voice of the Lord came unto him, saying:
>
> 13 — Lift up your head and be of good cheer; for behold, the time is at hand, and on this night shall the sign be given, and on the morrow come I into the world, to show unto the world that I will fulfil all that which I have caused to be spoken by the mouth of my holy prophets.
>
> 14 — Behold, I come unto my own, to fulfil all things which I have made known unto the children of men from the foundation of the world, and to do the will, both of the Father and of the Son—of the Father because of me, and of the Son because of my flesh. And behold, the time is at hand, and this night shall the sign be given.

When Christmas approaches, many families and congregations gather together to read scriptural accounts of the nativity story, especially from the Gospel of Luke. This remarkable account of Nephi's earnest prayer and the revelation he received just prior to the earthly birth of the Savior adds a powerful dimension and spiritual witness to the nativity story. These verses could just as well be read and shared at those Christmastime home evenings and sacrament meetings.

> 3 Nephi 1:29 — And there was also a cause of much sorrow among the Lamanites; for behold, they had many children who did grow up and began to wax strong in years, that they became for themselves, and were led away by some who were Zoramites, by their lyings and their flattering words, to join those Gadianton robbers.
>
> 30 — And thus were the Lamanites afflicted also, and began to decrease as to their faith and righteousness, because of the wickedness of the rising generation.

The phrase that sticks in the mind from this passage is "they became for themselves." By lying and flattering words, some members of the young generation of Lamanites became self-centered, leading them to decrease in faith and righteousness. We must be careful not to lead our young generation to "become for themselves." As parents and youth leaders, we must encourage their independence but at the same time encourage them and offer them opportunities to "become for others" through serving and sharing.

> 3 Nephi 9:14 — Yea, verily I say unto you, if ye will come unto me ye shall have eternal life. Behold, mine arm of mercy is extended towards you, and whosoever will come, him will I receive; and blessed are those who come unto me.
>
> 15 — Behold, I am Jesus Christ the Son of God. I created the heavens and the earth, and all things that in them are. I was with the Father from the beginning. I am in the Father, and the Father in me; and in me hath the Father glorified his name.
>
> 16 — I came unto my own, and my own received me not. And the scriptures concerning my coming are fulfilled.
>
> 17 — And as many as have received me, to them have I given to become the sons of God; and even so will I to as many as shall believe on my name, for behold, by me redemption cometh, and in me is the law of Moses fulfilled.
>
> 18 — I am the light and the life of the world. I am Alpha and Omega, the beginning and the end.

One of the most wonderful blessings of the Book of Mormon is to be able to read passages like this one in which the Lord himself delivers the message of His gospel. These words are living water straight from their eternal source, the "fount of every blessing."

> 19 — And ye shall offer up unto me no more the shedding of blood; yea, your sacrifices and your burnt offerings shall be done away, for I will accept none of

> your sacrifices and your burnt offerings.
>
> 20 — And ye shall offer for a sacrifice unto me a broken heart and a contrite spirit. And whoso cometh unto me with a broken heart and a contrite spirit, him will I baptize with fire and with the Holy Ghost, even as the Lamanites, because of their faith in me at the time of their conversion, were baptized with fire and with the Holy Ghost, and they knew it not.

The old sacrifices are no longer to be accepted. The Lord now requires a deeper sacrifice, the sacrifice of a broken heart and contrite spirit. This is a sacrifice that is supremely personal, a sacrifice that we cannot perform by merely going through the motions, whether those motions be bringing a lamb to the altar or dropping to our knees next to our beds and folding our arms in an attitude of prayer. If we do not go before the Lord humbly and sincerely, offering our very hearts, we are holding something back. We must give our all. We must give Him our hearts so that He can write His law on them. We must open our hearts to Him so that He can pour His pure love into them and make them whole once more.

> 21 — Behold, I have come unto the world to bring redemption unto the world, to save the world from sin.
>
> 22 — Therefore, whoso repenteth and cometh unto me as a little child, him will I receive, for of such is the kingdom of God. Behold, for such I have laid down my life, and have taken it up again; therefore repent, and come unto me ye ends of the earth, and be saved.

Note that the Lord says that He has come to save the world from sin. We often make a distinction between "the world," which has come to represent the unrighteous, unrepentant, unredeemed segment of creation, that segment of creation from which the righteous must separate themselves and Zion must flee, and "the kingdom," which we associate with the Church, Zion, the righteous, and of course, ourselves. But the Lord says He came to save the world—not the kingdom—from sin. As He said on another occasion, the healthy do not have need of a physician. The Lord is not merely the Lord of the kingdom, He is the master of all creation. He has come to save the world from sin.

Deep down, most of us realize that we really do live in the world, no matter how hard we try to align ourselves with the kingdom. Thank goodness we have a hope in Christ, He who came to save the world, to save us from the world, to save us from the devil, to save us from ourselves.

Will the entire world be saved? Clearly not. Does that diminish His power? No, because He will save all who come to Him in repentance. Some will choose to do so, some will choose otherwise. But He will judge all at the entrance to His kingdom, employing no servant there. He has all power over life and death, just as each of us has the agency to choose life or death. The Lord respects our agency; if we are to be saved, we must respect His infinite sacrifice by making our full but finite sacrifice of our broken heart and contrite spirit. Just as He condescended to come to the earth as a little child, so must we condescend to humble ourselves and become as little children before Him—humble, innocent, full of love, and eager to be taught of His ways.

Although this testimony of the Savior is given by His voice in revelation, soon He will appear in the flesh, the event to which the whole Book of Mormon has been building. As we read the Book of Mormon, working our way through hundreds of pages, we may well have already placed a mental bookmark in the eleventh chapter of 3 Nephi, for we know what it going to happen there.

> 3 Nephi 11:9 — And it came to pass that he stretched forth his hand and spake unto the people, saying:
>
> 10 — Behold, I am Jesus Christ, whom the prophets testified shall come into the world.
>
> 11 — And behold, I am the light and the life of the world; and I have drunk out of that bitter cup which the Father hath given me, and have glorified the Father in taking upon me the sins of the world, in the which I have suffered the will of the Father in all things from the beginning.

I do not know how many times I have read the Book of Mormon from beginning to end. I can testify honestly, though, that every time I work my way through the Book of Mormon and read these words, "Behold, I am Jesus Christ, whom the prophets testified shall come into the world," something happens deep within my soul. I am touched; I am humbled; I am grateful. For a few moments, I can read no further.

Moving on to verse 11, we encounter that magnificent declaration, "I am the light and life of the world." Having read all that has come before in the Book of Mormon, we are ready to accept that declaration as truth. We then stand humbled as we read the Savior's straightforward declaration of His mission to take upon Himself the sins of the world and thus do our Father's will to bring about our Father's glory, which we are comforted to know is to bring about the immortality and eternal life of man.

> 3 Nephi 11:30 — Behold, this is not my doctrine, to stir up the hearts of men with anger, one against another; but this is my doctrine, that such things should be done away.
>
> 31 — Behold, verily, verily, I say unto you, I will declare unto you my doctrine.
>
> 32 — And this is my doctrine, and it is the doctrine which the Father hath given unto me; and I bear record of the Father, and the Father beareth record of me, and the Holy Ghost beareth record of the Father and me; and I bear record that the Father commandeth all men, everywhere, to repent and believe in me.
>
> 33 — And whoso believeth in me, and is baptized, the same shall be saved; and they are they who shall inherit the kingdom of God.
>
> 34 — And whoso believeth not in me, and is not baptized, shall be damned.
>
> 35 — Verily, verily, I say unto you, that this is my doctrine, and I bear record of it from the Father; and whoso believeth in me believeth in the Father also; and unto him will the Father bear record of me, for he will visit him with fire and with the Holy Ghost.
>
> 36 — And thus will the Father bear record of me, and

the Holy Ghost will bear record unto him of the Father and me; for the Father, and I, and the Holy Ghost are one.

37 — And again I say unto you, ye must repent, and become as a little child, and be baptized in my name, or ye can in nowise receive these things.

38 — And again I say unto you, ye must repent, and be baptized in my name, and become as a little child, or ye can in nowise inherit the kingdom of God.

39 — Verily, verily, I say unto you, that this is my doctrine, and whoso buildeth upon this buildeth upon my rock, and the gates of hell shall not prevail against them.

40 — And whoso shall declare more or less than this, and establish it for my doctrine, the same cometh of evil, and is not built upon my rock; but he buildeth upon a sandy foundation, and the gates of hell stand open to receive such when the floods come and the winds beat upon them.

41 — Therefore, go forth unto this people, and declare the words which I have spoken, unto the ends of the earth.

Once again we can enjoy the great blessing the Book of Mormon affords us, the opportunity to hear the doctrine of Christ straight from the source. Faith, repentance, baptism, and the witness of the Holy Ghost undergird the true doctrine of Christ. This is the true foundation upon which we must build our lives, and as we do so, we must bear witness to the world of His goodness and mercy, teaching faith, repentance, and baptism to all.

3 Nephi 12:2 — And again, more blessed are they who shall believe in your words because that ye shall testify that ye have seen me, and that ye know that I am. Yea, blessed are they who shall believe in your words, and come down into the depths of humility and be baptized, for they shall be visited with fire and with the Holy Ghost, and shall receive a remission of their sins.

As chapter 12 opens, we read that after the Savior calls and sets apart the twelve who were commissioned to baptize in His name, He then turns to the gathered multitude and promises them that they will be blessed if they will heed the words of those disciples and be baptized. He further promises them the gift of the Holy Ghost.

He then pronounces another remarkable blessing. He promises the gathered multitude that those who will hear and believe in their testimonies will in turn be blessed with those same blessings with which the multitude had been blessed. In other words, the Savior blesses the multitude with the ability to bless others. He blesses them to be instruments in His hands through their examples and testimonies. Without calling them in so many words to be missionaries, He nevertheless calls them to be missionaries.

As we liken these verses unto ourselves, we can see that we have both the responsibility and the blessing of being witnesses for Christ. We have taken upon ourselves His name and we have promised to be witnesses of His power and mercy. By so doing, we can come to bless the lives of others as they hear our words and are led to their source, the Savior Himself, just as we were first led to the Savior through the words of our parents, our friends, or perhaps even complete strangers. The Savior has promised that those who hear His word will be blessed and also those who declare His word will be blessed.

> 3 Nephi 12:6 — And blessed are all they who do hunger and thirst after righteousness, for they shall be filled with the Holy Ghost.

As recorded in the Book of Mormon, the promise to those who hunger for righteousness is not just that they will be filled (as recorded in Matthew), but that they will be filled with the Holy Ghost. Having just a few verses ago promised those that would listen to His message that He would baptize them with fire and with the Holy Ghost, the Savior offers a promise that is backed up by the priesthood authority that He has bestowed.

> 3 Nephi 12:7 — And blessed are the merciful, for they shall obtain mercy.
>
> 8 — And blessed are all the pure in heart, for they shall see God.

Note how there is a feeling of progression in these verses. Those who hunger and thirst after righteousness can come unto Christ, be baptized, and be filled with the Holy Ghost. Those who have so humbled themselves come to grow more like Him, become more merciful and pure in heart as they come to have charity—the pure love of Christ—in their hearts. They are forgiven and forgiving. These are the Saints who are promised that they will see God. These verses bring to mind a similar promise given by the Savior in another context, speaking of the blessings of the temple:

> D&C 97:16 — Yea, and my presence shall be there, for I will come into it, and all the pure in heart that shall come into it shall see God.

From the promises recorded in Matthew through those recorded in 3 Nephi and then expanded upon in modern revelation, it should be clear that the Lord is eager to reveal Himself to those pure in heart who seek Him earnestly, and that the place to seek Him most earnestly is in the temple.

> 3 Nephi 12:19 — And behold, I have given you the law and the commandments of my Father, that ye shall believe in me, and that ye shall repent of your sins, and come unto me with a broken heart and a contrite spirit. Behold, ye have the commandments before you, and the law is fulfilled.
>
> 20 — Therefore come unto me and be ye saved; for verily I say unto you, that except ye shall keep my commandments, which I have commanded you at this time, ye shall in no case enter into the kingdom of heaven.

Once again the Savior expresses His basic message in a straightforward way. He is teaching us the commandments of His Father: we are commanded to have faith in Christ, to repent, and to keep the commandments. This is the way we stay on the strait and narrow path—by living faithfully, repentantly, and obediently. Likewise, we endure to the end by living each day faithfully, repentantly, and obediently, one day at a time, day after day, all the days of our life.

> 3 Nephi 12:48 — Therefore I would that ye should be perfect even as I, or your Father who is in heaven is perfect.

Now that Christ has been resurrected and shares full glory with His Father, He can add Himself to the famous injunction that we recall from Matthew. We need to follow His path and keep His commandments, just as He keeps the commandments of His Father.

> 3 Nephi 15:1 — And now it came to pass that when Jesus had ended these sayings he cast his eyes round about on the multitude, and said unto them: Behold, ye have heard the things which I taught before I ascended to my Father; therefore, whoso remembereth these sayings of mine and doeth them, him will I raise up at the last day.

As the Savior concludes His address, which closely parallels the Sermon on the Mount that is recorded in the New Testament, He reminds the assembled Nephite faithful that He has told them those things that He taught before His ascension. Christ was able to ascend to His Father because He had kept His Father's commandments; in like manner, we are enjoined to keep His commandments so that we too can be raised up.

> 3 Nephi 15:9 — Behold, I am the law, and the light. Look unto me, and endure to the end, and ye shall live; for unto him that endureth to the end will I give eternal life.
>
> 10 — Behold, I have given unto you the commandments; therefore keep my commandments. And this is the law and the prophets, for they truly testified of me.

The Savior teaches that He is the law and the light. The law shows us how to live, while the light gives us strength and hope, brightening our lives both figuratively and literally. The law shows us what we must do to endure to the end, while the light gives us the energy to do so. We must endure to the end in keeping the commandments, having a perfect brightness of hope, illuminated by the light of Christ, and a love for God and for others, keeping those two great commandments upon which hinge the law and the prophets.

> 3 Nephi 17:3 — Therefore, go ye unto your homes, and ponder upon the things which I have said, and ask of the Father, in my name, that ye may understand, and prepare your minds for the morrow, and I come unto you again.

As we read of the Lord instructing the Nephites to "ponder upon the things which I have said," so that they can prepare themselves to receive further instruction, we might well think of these words as a guide to our sacrament and temple worship. We need to go into our chapels and temples pondering those things we have learned from our study of the scriptures. We then need to leave our chapels and temples and go into our homes to ponder those things we have learned, turning once again to the scriptures to prepare ourselves for further learning in our chapels and temples.

> 3 Nephi 18:32 — Nevertheless, ye shall not cast him out of your synagogues, or your places of worship, for unto such shall ye continue to minister; for ye know not but what they will return and repent, and come unto me with full purpose of heart, and I shall heal them; and ye shall be the means of bringing salvation unto them.

Speaking of those who may be unworthy to fully partake of the sacrament, the Lord instructs His disciples that "unto such shall ye continue to minister." These words should serve us well today as a guide to our home and visiting teaching. Although many in our wards and branches seem to have simply given up on the Church, we must not give up on them, for we do not know who might be led to repent and be healed by the Lord. The Lord has not given up on us, despite His perfect knowledge of all our deepest flaws and sins; we must not give up on our less-active brothers and sisters, despite our superficial knowledge, suppositions, and imaginings concerning their apparent flaws and sins.

> 3 Nephi 23:1 — And now, behold, I say unto you,

> that ye ought to search these things. Yea, a commandment I give unto you that ye search these things diligently; for great are the words of Isaiah.

With tongue in cheek, I would observe that of all the verses in all of scripture, of all the warnings and thundering cries of impending destruction and imminent doom to be found in the written word, this particular verse may strike the greatest fear into the hearts of many Latter-day Saints, who can hardly bear to be reminded that they are under commandment to make a special study of the writings of the prophet Isaiah. "I'll pay my tithing," they think to themselves, "I'll be faithful to my spouse, I'll even do a little missionary work from time to time—but do I have to read and try to understand Isaiah?"

"Great are the words of Isaiah," testifies the Savior. If we will read the words of Isaiah as the Savior commanded, trying to put a little effort into it, or if nothing else, at least simply letting those poetic and noble words wash over us until they begin to sink in, perhaps we will begin to see what the Savior meant.

Remember, after all, that even the wicked priests of King Noah seemed to have searched diligently the words of Isaiah. If they could do it, so ought we, and our reading of the Book of Mormon should make it that much easier and enjoyable for us.

> 3 Nephi 23:14 — And now it came to pass that when Jesus had expounded all the scriptures in one, which they had written, he commanded them that they should teach the things which he had expounded unto them.

Note that once the Savior had ensured that the people had a more complete set of scriptures available, He then commanded that they should teach to each other what He had taught them. In our time, too, the Savior has given us an even more complete set of scriptures (the Book of Mormon, the Pearl of Great Price, the Doctrine and Covenants, plus the Joseph Smith translation of the Bible) and commanded that we use them to teach one another the doctrines of the gospel. The underlying principle seems to be that in teaching one another what the

Savior has taught us, we begin to internalize His teachings.

Reflect for a moment, for example, on how often the Lord has exhorted us to preach repentance. How much of that preaching about the importance of repentance is really meant for those we preach to, and how much is actually meant for those of us who have been called to preach it? I suspect the latter is actually the more significant. Not only must we learn to teach, but also we must teach to learn.

> 3 Nephi 27:13 — Behold I have given unto you my gospel, and this is the gospel which I have given unto you—that I came into the world to do the will of my Father, because my Father sent me.

The Savior summarizes His gospel by reiterating that He is doing the will of His Father. His Father sent Him to this earth so that He could be lifted up on the cross. In doing this, Christ submitted to the will of His Father and made it possible that all could be reconciled with God if they would repent, have faith, and follow His commandments.

> 3 Nephi 27:20 — Now this is the commandment: Repent, all ye ends of the earth, and come unto me and be baptized in my name, that ye may be sanctified by the reception of the Holy Ghost, that ye may stand spotless before me at the last day.
>
> 21 — Verily, verily, I say unto you, this is my gospel; and ye know the things that ye must do in my church; for the works which ye have seen me do that shall ye also do; for that which ye have seen me do even that shall ye do;
>
> 22 — Therefore, if ye do these things blessed are ye, for ye shall be lifted up at the last day.

Once again the Savior lays out in plain terms what is expected of those who seek salvation: they must repent, have faith in Christ, be baptized in His name, receive the gift of the Holy Ghost, and follow in His footsteps by doing those things that He did—serving, witnessing, and sacrificing. He spent His life in keeping the commandments and seeking to do the will of His Father, and so should we seek to keep the commandments and do the will of the Father and the Son under the inspiration of the Holy Ghost.

> 4 Nephi 1:3 — And they had all things common among them; therefore there were not rich and poor, bond and free, but they were all made free, and partakers of the heavenly gift.

The phrase that is usually remembered and discussed from this oft-quoted verse is "they had all things in common." We need to realize that in the natural state the Lord intended for us, we truly would have all things in common. The world has been put before us to share, the same world and the same blessings given to us all, but we have managed to divide things up through our own prideful nature.

When we come to see things this way—and we get a glimpse of it in the temple—we can see how it could be said of these people that "they were all made free." To live in such a way where we do not worry about getting and spending, but rather enjoy the blessings that we have been given and seek to share them with others, that is to live truly free. The temple shows us the way, but when we leave the temple, we tend to forget. We enter a world that, by and large, is completely unaware of the plan of happiness, a world in which money is the primary measure of worth, a world that is bound not by covenant but rather by convenience.

> 4 Nephi 1:16 — And there were no envyings, nor strifes, nor tumults, nor whoredoms, nor lyings, nor murders, nor any manner of lasciviousness; and surely there could not be a happier people among all the people who had been created by the hand of God.
>
> 17 — There were no robbers, nor murderers, neither were there Lamanites, nor any manner of -ites; but they were in one, the children of Christ, and heirs to the kingdom of God.

We certainly do not have this kind of unity in today's world. Do we have it in the Church? Do we have any "-ites" or "-ists," or are we truly all one people? Again, this is something that we catch a glimpse of in the temple, but when we leave the temple, we tend to fall back into the ways of the world. We all need each other, we all need the Church, and we all need the Lord. As we humble ourselves and repent, we will become a more unified and a happier people.

Chapter 9

Mormon

> Mormon 1:15 — And I, being fifteen years of age and being somewhat of a sober mind, therefore I was visited of the Lord, and tasted and knew of the goodness of Jesus.

Here is another unforgettably vivid phrase from the Book of Mormon, Mormon declaring that he "tasted and knew of the goodness of Jesus." Where it would have certainly been a strong and worthy testimony to say that he had heard or seen the goodness of the Lord, to say that he tasted the goodness of Jesus is so vivid, so intimate, and so compelling, that we cannot help but be moved by the power of Mormon's account.

Indeed, Mormon's writings about his own experiences are so vivid, so full of felicitous turns of phrase, that I cannot help but think that he must have had some sort of natural gift for writing. He apparently possessed just the sort of talent that would be needed to serve as the editor of a sacred record. But as vivid as his writing could be, it never seems to be self-serving. Mormon possessed not only great talent, but also great humility.

> Mormon 2:15 — And it came to pass that my sorrow did return unto me again, and I saw that the day of grace

> was passed with them, both temporally and spiritually; for I saw thousands of them hewn down in open rebellion against their God, and heaped up as dung upon the face of the land. And thus three hundred and forty and four years had passed away.

Here is another remarkable phrase: "I saw that the day of grace was passed with them, both temporally and spiritually." Mormon sounds as though he has thought deeply about these people of whom he goes on to write that he "saw thousands of them hewn down in open rebellion against their God, and heaped up as dung upon the face of the land." In this verse we find a mixture of the dispassionate and the intimate that truly captures our attention and makes us aware not only of the plight of this people but also of the reasons for it.

Mormon's use of the term "dung" is particularly telling. Seldom do we think of prophets using scatological terms to describe their people. This is direct and powerful language indeed.

> Mormon 3:12 — Behold, I had led them, notwithstanding their wickedness I had led them many times to battle, and had loved them, according to the love of God which was in me, with all my heart; and my soul had been poured out in prayer unto my God all the day long for them; nevertheless, it was without faith, because of the hardness of their hearts.

We can sense the intensity of Mormon's feelings as he reflects on what has happened. We can feel the power of his intellect as he crafts this sentence, which begins with rhythmic repetition, "Behold, I had led them, notwithstanding their wickedness I had led them many time to battle, and had loved them."

We can feel his anguish as he goes on to write that not only had he led them, but he "had loved them, according to the love of God which was in me, with all my heart." After testifying that he had poured out his soul in prayer in their behalf, he then makes the heartbreaking admission that "it was without faith." All the love of God in Mormon's heart was unable to overcome the hardness in the hearts of his people.

Sadly enough, Mormon knew this even as he led them many times in battle. How wrenching this must have been!

> Mormon 5:2 — But behold, I was without hope, for I knew the judgments of the Lord which should come upon them; for they repented not of their iniquities, but did struggle for their lives without calling upon that Being who created them.

Mormon has revealed that he has lost his faith in his people; even worse, he now writes, "I was without hope." Is he also without charity? No, he still has charity. We can feel the love in his heart as he writes of his despair in seeing his people destroying themselves through their iniquity.

> Mormon 5:17 — They were once a delightsome people, and they had Christ for their shepherd; yea, they were led even by God the Father.
>
> 18 — But now, behold, they are led about by Satan, even as chaff is driven before the wind, or as a vessel is tossed about upon the waves, without sail or anchor, or without anything wherewith to steer her; and even as she is, so are they.

Here we have the sad contrast of a people who have gone from Christ to Satan, from order to chaos, from walking the path to blowing in the wind or drifting on the sea. They have gone from the tree of life to the burning stubble. They have chosen death when they could have had life. How it must have hurt Mormon to see this once-delightsome people turn away from the Lord and wind up being heaped as dung upon the face of the land. Mormon employs this stark contrasting language to drive home the point to his readers that they must heed what happened to Mormon's people.

> Mormon 6:17 — O ye fair ones, how could ye have departed from the ways of the Lord! O ye fair ones, how could ye have rejected that Jesus, who stood with open arms to receive you!

Can you feel Mormon's pain as he writes "O ye fair ones?" This is one of the most haunting, wrenching verses in all of scripture. As we read it, we not only feel Mormon's pain, but we may reflect on the anguish we have felt when we have seen friends or loved ones—our fair ones—make wrong decisions and turn away from the Church and the Lord. We may also reflect on our own lives and vow that this will never be said of us by our friends and loved ones.

> Mormon 8:12 — And whoso receiveth this record, and shall not condemn it because of the imperfections which are in it, the same shall know of greater things than these. Behold, I am Moroni; and were it possible, I would make all things known unto you.

You shall know of greater things than these. Note that I did not enclose that sentence in quotation marks. As we read and study and ponder the Book of Mormon, we will rise above the imperfections in the text and the imperfections in ourselves to come to a deeper knowledge of and appreciation for our God and His great plan of happiness. This is one of the great promises of the Book of Mormon made by Moroni, who also makes other promises that are exciting to ponder.

> Mormon 9:11 — But behold, I will show unto you a God of miracles, even the God of Abraham, and the God of Isaac, and the God of Jacob; and it is that same God who created the heavens and the earth, and all things that in them are.

One of the remarkable things about the Book of Mormon is that it really does show us a God of miracles. Not miracles as people commonly seem to think of them—the turning of water into wine being chief among those that come to mind for most people—but rather the far greater miracles such as the miracle of faith, the miracle of repentance, the miracle of forgiveness, the miracle of mercy, and the miracle of the Atonement.

The miracles we have seen in individual lives, such as the repentance and forgiveness of Alma, are the truly mighty miracles. Those of us who have seen such miracles in our own lives or in the lives of those that we love are truly blessed. To be healed of our sickness by the power of the priesthood is certainly a miracle, but to be forgiven of our sins by the mercy of the Lord is a far greater miracle. Te be raised from the dead would be a mighty miracle, but to be raised from the dead and able to stand before our Lord without shame by virtue of His Atonement would be a far greater miracle.

> Mormon 9:27 — O then despise not, and wonder not, but hearken unto the words of the Lord, and ask the Father in the name of Jesus for what things soever ye shall stand in need. Doubt not, but be believing, and begin as in times of old, and come unto the Lord with all your heart, and work out your own salvation with fear and trembling before him.
>
> 28 — Be wise in the days of your probation; strip yourselves of all uncleanness; ask not, that ye may consume it on your lusts, but ask with a firmness unshaken, that ye will yield to no temptation, but that ye will serve the true and living God.
>
> 29 — See that ye are not baptized unworthily; see that ye partake not of the sacrament of Christ unworthily; but see that ye do all things in worthiness, and do it in the name of Jesus Christ, the Son of the living God; and if ye do this, and endure to the end, ye will in nowise be cast out.
>
> 30 — Behold, I speak unto you as though I spake from the dead; for I know that ye shall have my words.
>
> 31 — Condemn me not because of mine imperfection, neither my father, because of his imperfection, neither them who have written before him; but rather give thanks unto God that he hath made manifest unto you our imperfections, that ye may learn to be more wise than we have been.

Reaching out over the miles and centuries is this final advice from a prophet of olden times to us today. We are neither to look down upon nor just to wonder at the words of the Lord, but to integrate their counsel into our lives as we, on one hand, petition the Lord for those things we lack and, on the other hand, press forward faithfully and make an earnest, honest effort to obey the words of the Lord and work out our salvation. We know from the words of the Lord that we cannot save ourselves, but we also know that we ourselves must make the choice between salvation and damnation. We know that it is by grace that we are saved, but we also know that it is after all we can do. Thus we must strive to be worthy and endure to the end.

As we read the final two verses, we can sense the urgency and conviction that Moroni puts into his writing. He knows that we will have his words; as we read them, we become aware that we do indeed have them, and now the responsibility is upon us to ponder them and act upon them. Indeed, we now know that he knows we have his words, and as he and his father Mormon pressed on despite their imperfections, so must we. We now have a challenge and an obligation to learn from what Mormon and Moroni have given us and strive to be more wise than they were.

As much as we revere Mormon and Moroni, do we really think we can be more wise than they? That is the challenge that Moroni has passed on to us. We surely have much to ponder—and much to do.

Chapter 10

Ether

When we reach Ether, we know that we are getting close to the end of the Book of Mormon. We have seen the entire history of the Nephites and have observed how they went from a state of blessedness to a state of ruin and destruction because they did not remain faithful to their God. We can see this as a lesson for our civilization; we can also liken it unto ourselves and realize as individuals that our own futures will ultimately be determined by our faithfulness.

As we stop for a moment to ponder the fate of the Nephites, we prepare to read about the rise and fall of another civilization. While the story of the Nephites had been told over hundreds of pages, we know that the record of the Jaredites will be recounted in mere dozens of pages. The underlying message is much the same, just compressed in the interest of time. Moroni knows that he does not have much time left, but he has a story that he urgently wants us to read.

> Ether 1:1 — And now I, Moroni, proceed to give an account of those ancient inhabitants who were destroyed by the hand of the Lord upon the face of this north country.

Once again we have a book in the Book of Mormon beginning with the author's declaration of his identity; in this case, it is "I, Moroni . . ." Phrases such as this seem to give a rhythm and feeling of continuity to the work.

We also come to realize that the whole Book of Mormon is something that Moroni has prepared for us, taking over from his father, Mormon. Indeed, the Book of Mormon bears not only Mormon's name, but also his son Moroni's personal stamp. As we contemplate this, we begin to appreciate more fully Moroni's important role in visiting and teaching the young Joseph Smith so that the record that Moroni had sealed up could come forth in the latter days.

> Ether 1:33 — Which Jared came forth with his brother and their families, with some others and their families, from the great tower, at the time the Lord confounded the language of the people, and swore in his wrath that they should be scattered upon all the face of the earth; and according to the word of the Lord the people were scattered.

Here we have our first glimpse of Jared and the more well-known Book of Mormon figure mentioned in the record only as "the brother of Jared." The latter turns out to be, as those who have read the Book of Mormon before well know, one of the more memorable figures in all of scripture. Although it was Jared himself who wound up with a people and a book named after him, it was his unnamed brother who is actually at the center of the story.

> Ether 1:34 — And the brother of Jared being a large and mighty man, and a man highly favored of the Lord, Jared, his brother, said unto him: Cry unto the Lord, that he will not confound us that we may not understand our words.
>
> 35 — And it came to pass that the brother of Jared did cry unto the Lord, and the Lord had compassion upon Jared; therefore he did not confound the language of Jared; and Jared and his brother were not confounded.

Reading these verses, I cannot help but think of that favorite hymn phrase, "Did you think to pray?" And in fairness to Jared, note that it is he who is here portrayed as the quicker thinker, urging his "highly favored" brother to petition the Lord in their behalf.

We can surely think of situations today wherein a priesthood leader who is highly favored by the Lord, such as a righteous bishop or stake president, has in a time of crisis been prompted by a counselor to petition the Lord for guidance. Closer to home, there are countless examples where the righteous and favored Relief Society president has been prompted by her husband to seek guidance from the Lord, or where a proud husband has been so counseled by his good wife.

> Ether 1:36 — Then Jared said unto his brother: Cry again unto the Lord, and it may be that he will turn away his anger from them who are our friends, that he confound not their language.

Jared now follows the pattern we have encountered so often in the Book of Mormon: if we have been richly blessed, let's not forget our friends. As we see this pattern repeated over and over again, surely we must come to see that it is something the Lord is trying to emphasize to us. Surely He is using these examples to show us that as He has loved us, as He as blessed us, so we must love, bless, and pray for one another.

> Ether 1:41 — Go to and gather together thy flocks, both male and female, of every kind; and also of the seed of the earth of every kind; and thy families; and also Jared thy brother and his family; and also thy friends and their families, and the friends of Jared and their families.

Here we see a pattern much like that found in the Bible regarding Noah. It is a time when the land is going to have to be repopulated, so those in charge of the new land are told to gather animals and plants so that life can be carried on. As God populated the earth, so now will His servants populate this new land. Note how at the outset of Ether we have a kind of brief retelling of, or at least a strong allusion to, the creation story.

> Ether 2:3 — And they did also carry with them deseret, which, by interpretation, is a honey bee; and thus they did

> carry with them swarms of bees, and all manner of that which was upon the face of the land, seeds of every kind.

The honeybee will ensure that seeds are propagated. The honeybee is a living symbol of fertility and industriousness, qualities that are needed to build up and sustain a civilization in a new and strange land.

> Ether 2:8 — And he had sworn in his wrath unto the brother of Jared, that whoso should possess this land of promise, from that time henceforth and forever, should serve him, the true and only God, or they should be swept off when the fulness of his wrath should come upon them.
>
> 9 — And now, we can behold the decrees of God concerning this land, that it is a land of promise; and whatsoever nation shall possess it shall serve God, or they shall be swept off when the fulness of his wrath shall come upon them. And the fulness of his wrath cometh upon them when they are ripened in iniquity.

The phrase "and now, we can behold" serves as our familiar Book of Mormon alert that we are being taught a lesson that Moroni (and by implication, the Lord) believes is of vital importance for us to absorb. The direct lesson is that this land is a land of promise in which those who obey the Lord will prosper but those who turn away from the Lord will fall. The indirect lesson that we can learn from likening this scripture unto ourselves is that this mortal condition is a life of promise in which we will prosper and attain salvation if we seek and follow the Lord or have our promise swept away if we choose to turn away from His counsels. As a nation or as individuals, the choice is ours.

> Ether 2:11 — And this cometh unto you, O ye Gentiles, that ye may know the decrees of God—that ye may repent, and not continue in your iniquities until the fulness come, that ye may not bring down the fulness of the wrath of God upon you as the inhabitants of the land have hitherto done.

When as a teenager I first read the phrase "O ye Gentiles," I was myself a Gentile. Of course, I did not think of myself as Gentile, but thank goodness I was able to be serious about my reading of the Book of Mormon to the point that I was able to gain a testimony. When we hesitate to give a copy of the Book of Mormon to a friend, remember that in large part it was written expressly for those who are not members of the church.

> Ether 2:14 — And it came to pass at the end of four years that the Lord came again unto the brother of Jared, and stood in a cloud and talked with him. And for the space of three hours did the Lord talk with the brother of Jared, and chastened him because he remembered not to call upon the name of the Lord.

Some of us may remember times in our lives when we have spent perhaps fifteen or twenty minutes in bishops' offices being chastened, but can any of us really imagine what it would be like to spend three hours with the Lord being chastened? What an experience that must have been! As we read on, we see that this interview had quite an effect on the brother of Jared, whose subsequent encounters with the Lord were far more positive.

> Ether 2:15 — And the brother of Jared repented of the evil which he had done, and did call upon the name of the Lord for his brethren who were with him. And the Lord said unto him: I will forgive thee and thy brethren of their sins; but thou shalt not sin any more, for ye shall remember that my Spirit will not always strive with man; wherefore, if ye will sin until ye are fully ripe ye shall be cut off from the presence of the Lord. And these are my thoughts upon the land which I shall give you for your inheritance; for it shall be a land choice above all other lands.

Note once again an instance where one repents and is forgiven and then prays for his brethren, who are in turn forgiven. "My spirit will not always strive with man" is what Jared and his brethren are then warned, a warning that we would do well to heed today. Those with whom the Spirit no longer strives are those who are lost.

> Ether 3:14 — Behold, I am he who was prepared from the foundation of the world to redeem my people. Behold, I am Jesus Christ. I am the Father and the Son. In me shall all mankind have life, and that eternally, even they who shall believe on my name; and they shall become my sons and my daughters.

Having been chastened by the Lord, the brother of Jared now has the unimaginable experience of having the Lord declare directly to him in unequivocal terms, "Behold, I am Jesus Christ." Again, can we imagine such an experience happening to us?

To liken this scripture to ourselves from another perspective, we might also imagine what we could declare to the Lord in unequivocal terms. That we have sinned, that we are dependent upon His mercy, that we know He is the Christ—these are chief among the things that we could and must declare to Him unequivocally.

The Lord has put mechanisms in place whereby we may be trained in that regard. Each week we are given the opportunity to partake of the sacrament and declare our willingness to follow Him and take His name upon us. In the temple, we make solemn covenants that bind us to Him, and we have the opportunity to be reminded of those covenants each time we return to the temple to serve as proxy for those who are dead. And we know that eventually we will have our own audience with Him, the Keeper of the Gate, when we will fully recognize Him and acknowledge Him as Jesus Christ, the Holy One of Israel, our Lord and Savior.

> Ether 3:19 — And because of the knowledge of this man he could not be kept from beholding within the veil; and he saw the finger of Jesus, which, when he saw, he fell with fear; for he knew that it was the finger of the Lord; and he had faith no longer, for he knew, nothing doubting.

This is a simply remarkable verse. We are told that the brother of

Jared "could not be kept from beholding within the veil" because of his knowledge, but then we immediately see that knowledge increase dramatically, as he sees the finger of the Lord and falls with fear because he knows it is the Lord that he is encountering. As the text so plainly but dramatically explains, "He had faith no longer, for he knew, nothing doubting." We have seen knowledge added upon knowledge, and faith transcended.

> Ether 3:20 — Wherefore, having this perfect knowledge of God, he could not be kept from within the veil; therefore he saw Jesus; and he did minister unto him.
>
> 21 — And it came to pass that the Lord said unto the brother of Jared: Behold, thou shalt not suffer these things which ye have seen and heard to go forth unto the world, until the time cometh that I shall glorify my name in the flesh; wherefore, ye shall treasure up the things which ye have seen and heard, and show it to no man.

Verse 20 is like verse 19 greatly amplified. In verse 19, the brother of Jared's knowledge let him peer within the veil, while in verse 20, his perfect knowledge lets him not just behold that which was within the veil, but lets him enter within the veil, where he sees and is taught by the Lord Himself. He then receives the divine counsel to "treasure up the things which ye have seen and heard, and show it to no man."

When particularly sacred knowledge is given to mortals, it is often the case that they are counseled to keep this knowledge to themselves. Moses and Abraham, for example, were given great knowledge. Not all of it were they privileged to record directly in their written accounts. The complete knowledge they were given was treasure that they kept in their own hearts and minds, but it undoubtedly sustained their faith, informed their writings, enriched their lives, and inspired their service.

For those of us who have been to the temple and received our endowment, the same counsel applies. We too have been given great knowledge that we have been counseled to treasure within ourselves and not share with the world. Although we do not openly share this knowledge with others, if we are faithful to our covenants, the knowledge we have been given in the temple surely sustains our faith, informs our expression, enriches our lives, and inspires our service.

> Ether 3:25 — And when the Lord had said these words, he showed unto the brother of Jared all the inhabitants of the earth which had been, and also all that would be; and he withheld them not from his sight, even unto the ends of the earth.
>
> 26 — For he had said unto him in times before, that if he would believe in him that he could show unto him all things—it should be shown unto him; therefore the Lord could not withhold anything from him, for he knew that the Lord could show him all things.

As it was with Moses and Abraham, the whole plan is revealed to the brother of Jared. All the inhabitants of the earth, past and future, are shown to him. As we come into the church and grow in the gospel, possibilities begin to open up for us. As we learn of the plan of salvation, that great plan of happiness, we begin to see those who have come before us and we begin to catch the vision of the kingdoms yet before us. As we stand before the mirrors in the sealing room of the temple, we begin to catch the vision of the generations behind us and the generations yet to come. The Lord lays this all out so that we can see both who we are and whom we serve.

> Ether 4:5 — Wherefore the Lord hath commanded me to write them; and I have written them. And he commanded me that I should seal them up; and he also hath commanded that I should seal up the interpretation thereof; wherefore I have sealed up the interpreters, according to the commandment of the Lord.
>
> 6 — For the Lord said unto me: They shall not go forth unto the Gentiles until the day that they shall repent of their iniquity, and become clean before the Lord.
>
> 7 — And in that day that they shall exercise faith in me, saith the Lord, even as the brother of Jared did, that they may become sanctified in me, then will I manifest unto them the things which the brother of Jared saw, even

> to the unfolding unto them all my revelations, saith Jesus Christ, the Son of God, the Father of the heavens and of the earth, and all things that in them are.

The Lord instructs Moroni to take the full record of the things revealed to the brother of Jared and "seal them up." Only when men and women have sufficient faith will the Lord allow these teachings to come forth. We can interpret the meaning of these verses in at least two ways: first, that at some future time when people have great faith the record will be translated and disseminated; second, that as individuals develop great faith, they will be taught of Christ and learn those doctrines that the brother of Jared was taught.

These two lines of interpretation need not be seen as mutually exclusive. Today, we can exercise faith by attending to our scripture study and temple worship. In so doing, we may come to learn many of the things that the brother of Jared was no doubt taught about the Savior. At the same time, we can look forward in faith toward a future time when more of the record will be revealed and we may receive a less abridged version of the Book of Ether.

> Ether 4:12 — And whatsoever thing persuadeth men to do good is of me; for good cometh of none save it be of me. I am the same that leadeth men to all good; he that will not believe my words will not believe me—that I am; and he that will not believe me will not believe the Father who sent me. For behold, I am the Father, I am the light, and the life, and the truth of the world.
>
> 13 — Come unto me, O ye Gentiles, and I will show unto you the greater things, the knowledge which is hid up because of unbelief.
>
> 14 — Come unto me, O ye house of Israel, and it shall be made manifest unto you how great things the Father hath laid up for you, from the foundation of the world; and it hath not come unto you, because of unbelief.
>
> 15 — Behold, when ye shall rend that veil of unbelief which doth cause you to remain in your awful state of wickedness, and hardness of heart, and blindness of mind,

> then shall the great and marvelous things which have been hid up from the foundation of the world from you—yea, when ye shall call upon the Father in my name, with a broken heart and a contrite spirit, then shall ye know that the Father hath remembered the covenant which he made unto your fathers, O house of Israel.
>
> 16 — And then shall my revelations which I have caused to be written by my servant John be unfolded in the eyes of all the people. Remember, when ye see these things, ye shall know that the time is at hand that they shall be made manifest in very deed.
>
> 17 — Therefore, when ye shall receive this record ye may know that the work of the Father has commenced upon all the face of the land.
>
> 18 — Therefore, repent all ye ends of the earth, and come unto me, and believe in my gospel, and be baptized in my name; for he that believeth and is baptized shall be saved; but he that believeth not shall be damned; and signs shall follow them that believe in my name.
>
> 19 — And blessed is he that is found faithful unto my name at the last day, for he shall be lifted up to dwell in the kingdom prepared for him from the foundation of the world. And behold it is I that hath spoken it. Amen.

Once again we are reminded that the Savior is the source of good. He promised that if we are faithful and humble, great knowledge will be ours. We are taught that things now hidden will be revealed to us if we exercise humble faith in Christ. Great knowledge is to come forth to those who repent.

Once again (as in 1 Nephi 14:18–27), reference is made to the record of the Apostle John. Surely this should be an incentive to us to study the gospel and other writings of that beloved visionary who testified so forcefully of the Savior.

> Ether 6:17 — And they were taught to walk humbly before the Lord; and they were also taught from on high.

Although this is something of an inconspicuous little verse that contains no bold doctrine, when I read through the Book of Mormon this time around I could not help but be struck by the vivid contrast implicit in these words. They were taught to walk humbly, which means to make themselves low to the ground, yet they were taught from on high. We can see this as another type of manifestation of the condescension of God.

How often in the scriptures have we seen that those who humble themselves, who make themselves low, are lifted by the Lord? How often were those who had truly humbled themselves told to seek the Lord in a high place, at the top of a mountain? Even today, we are taught to be humble and to go to the temple, our latter-day mountain of the Lord, to be endowed from on high.

> Ether 6:22 — And it came to pass that the people desired of them that they should anoint one of their sons to be a king over them.
>
> 23 — And now behold, this was grievous unto them. And the brother of Jared said unto them: Surely this thing leadeth into captivity.

The perils of having a king are familiar to students of the Old Testament. The record of the Nephites also testifies to these perils; noble leaders such as King Benjamin are the exception, not the rule. The brother of Jared surely was prescient and inspired in his observation.

> Ether 7:20 — And the country was divided; and there were two kingdoms, the kingdom of Shule, and the kingdom of Cohor, the son of Noah.

First the people get a king, then the kingdom is divided. We know from our study of the scriptures to recognize this pattern. We also know that no real good will come from it, but rather enmity and strife. In his abridgment of the record, Moroni wants to be sure that this point is driven home.

> Ether 8:9 — Now the daughter of Jared was exceedingly fair. And it came to pass that she did talk with her father, and said unto him: Whereby hath my father

> so much sorrow? Hath he not read the record which our fathers brought across the great deep? Behold, is there not an account concerning them of old, that they by their secret plans did obtain kingdoms and great glory?

When we think about the record that must have been brought with the Jaredites, we would think that there must have been much more contained therein than an account of those who used secret plans for evil purposes. There must have been a account of the creation, of our first parents, and of the goodness of God. Surely there would have been mention of the need for obedience and sacrifice. But the allure of obtaining kingdoms and great glory was most seductive.

> Ether 8:15 — And it came to pass that thus they did agree with Akish. And Akish did administer unto them the oaths which were given by them of old who also sought power, which had been handed down even from Cain, who was a murderer from the beginning.

Once again we read of these secrets handed down from Cain (Master Mahan)—who received them from whom? Cain received them straight from the source, the Father of Lies. If one can murder to get gain, then one can do anything for any reason. One can lie to get gain. One can torture to get gain. One can terrorize to get gain. The possibilities for evil become infinite. Thus the Atonement needed to be based on an infinite sacrifice.

> Ether 8:26 — Wherefore, I, Moroni, am commanded to write these things that evil may be done away, and that the time may come that Satan may have no power upon the hearts of the children of men, but that they may be persuaded to do good continually, that they may come unto the fountain of all righteousness and be saved.

The Book of Mormon gives us a strong witness of the magnificent saving power of the Atonement. After writing of the evils perpetrated by men as the result of their succumbing to the great temptation for glory and power originally revealed to Cain by Satan himself, Moroni writes of the power of Christ to bring goodness into the hearts of men. Reflecting on Moroni's words, we can see that his life has followed the pattern of faith, hope, and charity. Through the faith he learned from his father, he has hope in Christ and hope for the distant future—even though the immediate future is bleak—and a love God and of all men and women, which is true charity. Because of the pure love of Christ that is in his heart, he is writing that we might be touched by his words.

Moroni then gives us a broad overview of some general spiritual ups and downs in chapters 9 and 10. Writing of a king named Emer in chapter 9, Moroni records something quite remarkable:

> Ether 9:21 — And Emer did execute judgment in righteousness all his days, and he begat many sons and daughters; and he begat Coriantum, and he anointed Coriantum to reign in his stead.
>
> 22 — And after he had anointed Coriantum to reign in his stead he lived four years, and he saw peace in the land; yea, and he even saw the Son of Righteousness, and did rejoice and glory in his day; and he died in peace.

After ruling righteously and retiring from public life, Emer sees the Lord. Here is a man that we hear very little about, yet it is recorded that he beheld the Savior. Moroni has perhaps recorded this for us so that we can see that even in the midst of turmoil and strife, if we can live our own lives in righteousness, we can have a bright hope in Christ, who will never forsake us.

> Ether 11:8 — And the people began to repent of their iniquity; and inasmuch as they did the Lord did have mercy on them.

Here we have yet another small verse with a big message: repentance brings mercy. If we will humble ourselves and repent, the Lord will forgive us. We need to be reminded over and over again who God is and what we can and must be. God is merciful, and we can be forgiven. God is forgiving, and we must be forgiving.

Ether 12:6 — And now, I, Moroni, would speak somewhat concerning these things; I would show unto the world that faith is things which are hoped for and not seen; wherefore, dispute not because ye see not, for ye receive no witness until after the trial of your faith.

7 — For it was by faith that Christ showed himself unto our fathers, after he had risen from the dead; and he showed not himself unto them until after they had faith in him; wherefore, it must needs be that some had faith in him, for he showed himself not unto the world.

8 — But because of the faith of men he has shown himself unto the world, and glorified the name of the Father, and prepared a way that thereby others might be partakers of the heavenly gift, that they might hope for those things which they have not seen.

9 — Wherefore, ye may also have hope, and be partakers of the gift, if ye will but have faith.

10 — Behold it was by faith that they of old were called after the holy order of God.

11 — Wherefore, by faith was the law of Moses given. But in the gift of his Son hath God prepared a more excellent way; and it is by faith that it hath been fulfilled.

12 — For if there be no faith among the children of men God can do no miracle among them; wherefore, he showed not himself until after their faith.

13 — Behold, it was the faith of Alma and Amulek that caused the prison to tumble to the earth.

14 — Behold, it was the faith of Nephi and Lehi that wrought the change upon the Lamanites, that they were baptized with fire and with the Holy Ghost.

15 — Behold, it was the faith of Ammon and his brethren which wrought so great a miracle among the Lamanites.

16 — Yea, and even all they who wrought miracles wrought them by faith, even those who were before Christ and also those who were after.

17 — And it was by faith that the three disciples

> obtained a promise that they should not taste of death; and they obtained not the promise until after their faith.
>
> 18 — And neither at any time hath any wrought miracles until after their faith; wherefore they first believed in the Son of God.
>
> 19 — And there were many whose faith was so exceedingly strong, even before Christ came, who could not be kept from within the veil, but truly saw with their eyes the things which they had beheld with an eye of faith, and they were glad.
>
> 20 — And behold, we have seen in this record that one of these was the brother of Jared; for so great was his faith in God, that when God put forth his finger he could not hide it from the sight of the brother of Jared, because of his word which he had spoken unto him, which word he had obtained by faith.
>
> 21 — And after the brother of Jared had beheld the finger of the Lord, because of the promise which the brother of Jared had obtained by faith, the Lord could not withhold anything from his sight; wherefore he showed him all things, for he could no longer be kept without the veil.

In these verses Moroni extols the virtues of faith. We learn not only about faith, but also about Moroni. Clearly, he was writing these words after carefully reading and pondering those things that had been written upon the plates entrusted to him by his father. Clearly, he had read the records of both the Nephites and the Jaredites and had learned much from them. In so doing, and through his own experience, he had come to a profound understanding of the nature of and necessity for faith in Christ.

When Moroni writes that "ye receive no witness until after the trial of your faith," we can sense that this is no mere intellectual declaration, but rather a solemn witness born by one who has had his faith tried by the awful scenes he has witnessed. We also sense the urgency with which he writes as he quickly reels off example after example of the power of faith. He wants us to ponder these things for ourselves, not merely to take his word for it, but to search for ourselves within the scriptures for accounts of those who have overcome great obstacles and participated in mighty miracles through the power of their faith, so that we ourselves will develop a deeper and more abiding faith that can serve as a firm foundation when the winds of destruction blow over us.

Finally, he wants us to catch the vision that there is more to be seen than we see at first. If we can exercise faith sufficient to see even the finger of the Lord, then we can behold the truth of all things. If we can exercise faith sufficient to see the hand of the Lord in our lives, then we can come to see the great plan of happiness in its entirety, and fully appreciate our role in bringing about the purposes of the Lord.

> Ether 12:26 — And when I had said this, the Lord spake unto me, saying: Fools mock, but they shall mourn; and my grace is sufficient for the meek, that they shall take no advantage of your weakness;
>
> 27 — And if men come unto me I will show unto them their weakness. I give unto men weakness that they may be humble; and my grace is sufficient for all men that humble themselves before me; for if they humble themselves before me, and have faith in me, then will I make weak things become strong unto them.
>
> 28 — Behold, I will show unto the Gentiles their weakness, and I will show unto them that faith, hope and charity bringeth unto me—the fountain of all righteousness.
>
> 29 — And I, Moroni, having heard these words, was comforted, and said: O Lord, thy righteous will be done, for I know that thou workest unto the children of men according to their faith;
>
> 30 — For the brother of Jared said unto the mountain Zerin, Remove—and it was removed. And if he had not had faith it would not have moved; wherefore thou workest after men have faith.

Once more we have a discussion in the Book of Mormon that centers around the necessity of and relationship among faith, hope, and charity—but this time around, the concept of weakness is added to the discussion. Moroni reports that the Lord revealed to him that human beings are given weaknesses and shown their weaknesses to humble them. Humility leads to repentance, and then to faith, hope, and charity as those who are repentant are led closer to Christ.

For those who look at their weakness as a curse, though, or as an excuse, humility will not follow. Weaknesses will remain weaknesses and hearts will remain hard. It will be difficult to come to Christ under those circumstances, as much more repentance will be required of those who are hard of heart.

The Book of Mormon teaches repeatedly the pattern of humility, repentance, faith, hope, and charity. Indeed, Ether 12:28 can plausibly be interpreted as referring to this central teaching in the Book of Mormon coming forth to the Gentiles through the very mechanism of the Book of Mormon.

> Ether 12:34 — And now I know that this love which thou hast had for the children of men is charity; wherefore, except men shall have charity they cannot inherit that place which thou hast prepared in the mansions of thy Father.

In this fascinating verse, Moroni underscores for us the necessity of charity. As we have been taught previously (for example, 2 Nephi 26:30), charity is not just something that is nice to have, it is something that we must have, and we have been commanded to seek for it. What is particularly striking here is how Moroni, in addressing the Savior, recognizes and acknowledges that the love of Christ is charity, while at the same moment comprehending why it is that men and women must come to have charity. To dwell with Christ, we must have His love in our hearts. It is no accident that the first two great commandments are commandments to love, nor is it a mere literary device when John declares that God is love and that we love Him because

He first loved us (1 John 4:8, 19). As we seek to love God and love our neighbor, we feel the love of God and the pure love of Christ takes root in us. We are humbled by His great gift and begin to grow in faith, hope, and charity.

Chapter 11

Moroni

When we finish reading about the tragic end of the Jaredites, complete with accounts of brutal, senseless hand-to-hand combat, we begin to see what Moroni is trying to pass on to us. In the Book of Ether, Moroni's own voice emerges from the text that he is compiling, urging us to learn from the mistakes of the past and testifying to us that our only hope lies in Christ.

Now that he has completed compiling and abridging the records of the distant past, Moroni turns to his final task, compiling and recording some of the ordinances of the Church and passing along some of the final thoughts of his father, Mormon. He then seizes the opportunity to add his final, personal, impassioned testimony of Christ before he seals the record up for the last time.

Those of us who have read the Book of Mormon before look forward to reading Moroni, not just because it marks the end point of our reading, but because we know what a powerful and inspiring message it contains. As we read the words of Moroni, we know that what we have read in the Book of Mormon is crucial to our salvation. We know that the message of the Book of Mormon is something to be both savored and shared.

> Moroni 1:3 — And I, Moroni, will not deny the Christ; wherefore, I wander whithersoever I can for the safety of mine own life.

After all he has been through, after being so discouraged by his people, Moroni makes his simple and strong declaration, "I will not deny the Christ." As we reflect on this passage, our thoughts may well be drawn to the passage in section 76 of the Doctrine and Covenants, wherein those in the Terrestrial Kingdom are characterized as not having been valiant in their testimony of the Savior. Moroni is valiant. As we come to appreciate just how valiant he is, our resolve to heed his counsel is strengthened. Such is the power of righteous example and heartfelt testimony.

> Moroni 2:1 — The words of Christ, which he spake unto his disciples, the twelve whom he had chosen, as he laid his hands upon them—
>
> 2 — And he called them by name, saying: Ye shall call on the Father in my name, in mighty prayer; and after ye have done this ye shall have power that to him upon whom ye shall lay your hands, ye shall give the Holy Ghost; and in my name shall ye give it, for thus do mine apostles.
>
> 3 — Now Christ spake these words unto them at the time of his first appearing; and the multitude heard it not, but the disciples heard it; and on as many as they laid their hands, fell the Holy Ghost.

In these closing chapters of the Book of Mormon, Moroni passes along some instructions about how things ought to be done in the church, instructions that originated with the Lord Himself and then were passed down through generations of priesthood leaders. The gift of the Holy Ghost is a vital part of the true church, the means by which comfort, counsel, and testimony are imparted to the members.

> Moroni 3:1 — The manner which the disciples, who were called the elders of the church, ordained priests and teachers—
>
> 2 — After they had prayed unto the Father in the name of Christ, they laid their hands upon them, and said:

> 3 — In the name of Jesus Christ I ordain you to be a priest, (or, if he be a teacher) I ordain you to be a teacher, to preach repentance and remission of sins through Jesus Christ, by the endurance of faith on his name to the end. Amen.
>
> 4 — And after this manner did they ordain priests and teachers, according to the gifts and callings of God unto men; and they ordained them by the power of the Holy Ghost, which was in them.

We sometimes tend to gloss over these passages about ordination; after all, we know very well how priests and teachers are to be ordained. It might profit us, though, to take a moment to reflect that the reason these brethren are ordained to the priesthood is to teach repentance and remission of sins along with the principle of enduring to the end. These are hardly trivial things; indeed they are the core elements of the gospel of Jesus Christ, and they are to be taught by the priesthood.

As we contemplate the responsibilities of the priesthood and reflect upon the necessity of our enduring in faith on the name of Christ, we are ready to focus on what is really being said in our sacrament prayers, which in our day typically are offered by young men who are ordained as priests in the Aaronic Priesthood. Although these young men hold what we refer to as the "lesser" priesthood, they play a vital role in reminding us of the covenants we have taken upon ourselves as members of the Church of Jesus Christ. In reading the Book of Mormon, one of the final things we are privileged to do is to take the opportunity to read and reflect upon the sacrament prayers.

> Moroni 4:3 — O God, the Eternal Father, we ask thee in the name of thy Son, Jesus Christ, to bless and sanctify this bread to the souls of all those who partake of it; that they may eat in remembrance of the body of thy Son, and witness unto thee, O God, the Eternal Father, that they are willing to take upon them the name of thy Son, and always remember him, and keep his commandments which he

> hath given them, that they may always have his Spirit to be with them. Amen.

In the prayer on the bread, we witness that we are willing to take upon us the name of Jesus Christ. We relive the experience of the faithful who heard the words of King Benjamin so many centuries before, and we confirm our desire to press forward along that strait and narrow path.

> Moroni 5:2 — O God, the Eternal Father, we ask thee, in the name of thy Son, Jesus Christ, to bless and sanctify this wine to the souls of all those who drink of it, that they may do it in remembrance of the blood of thy Son, which was shed for them; that they may witness unto thee, O God, the Eternal Father, that they do always remember him, that they may have his Spirit to be with them. Amen.

In the prayer on the water, we remember the blood of Christ, which dripped for us at Golgotha and gushed for us at Calvary, that blood which washes away our sins. We can contemplate that paradoxical promise of having our garments being washed clean and white by that bright red blood.

> Moroni 6:1 — And now I speak concerning baptism. Behold, elders, priests, and teachers were baptized; and they were not baptized save they brought forth fruit meet that they were worthy of it.
>
> 2 — Neither did they receive any unto baptism save they came forth with a broken heart and a contrite spirit, and witnessed unto the church that they truly repented of all their sins.
>
> 3 — And none were received unto baptism save they took upon them the name of Christ, having a determination to serve him to the end.
>
> 4 — And after they had been received unto baptism, and were wrought upon and cleansed by the power of the Holy Ghost, they were numbered among the people of

> the church of Christ; and their names were taken, that they might be remembered and nourished by the good word of God, to keep them in the right way, to keep them continually watchful unto prayer, relying alone upon the merits of Christ, who was the author and the finisher of their faith.
>
> 5 — And the church did meet together oft, to fast and to pray, and to speak one with another concerning the welfare of their souls.
>
> 6 — And they did meet together oft to partake of bread and wine, in remembrance of the Lord Jesus.

In these verses, Moroni provides an overview of the basic order of the church in his day, similar to what is spelled out for us in our day in section 20 of the Doctrine and Covenants. Once more, we read in the Book of Mormon that those who followed Christ met together often to fast and pray. As we read the Book of Mormon, we are reminded of the importance of fasting and prayer. As we think to pray, do we think to fast?

> Moroni 6:7 — And they were strict to observe that there should be no iniquity among them; and whoso was found to commit iniquity, and three witnesses of the church did condemn them before the elders, and if they repented not, and confessed not, their names were blotted out, and they were not numbered among the people of Christ.
>
> 8 — But as oft as they repented and sought forgiveness, with real intent, they were forgiven.

One of the central teachings of the Book of Mormon is forgiveness. Over and over again we read of instances where people repent and are immediately forgiven by the Lord. These verses, in which Moroni passes on to us the teachings of his father, Mormon, emphasize that in the Lord's church, forgiveness for one another must be practiced. How often can we be forgiven? As often as we sincerely repent. How often must we forgive even those who we know without doubt have transgressed? As often as they sincerely repent.

And how will we know that they have repented sincerely? For that, we must have the Spirit; to have the Spirit, we must be humble and repentant ourselves.

We love the Lord because He first loved us. We forgive others because the Lord first forgave us.

> Moroni 7:11 — For behold, a bitter fountain cannot bring forth good water; neither can a good fountain bring forth bitter water; wherefore, a man being a servant of the devil cannot follow Christ; and if he follow Christ he cannot be a servant of the devil.
>
> 12 — Wherefore, all things which are good cometh of God; and that which is evil cometh of the devil; for the devil is an enemy unto God, and fighteth against him continually, and inviteth and enticeth to sin, and to do that which is evil continually.
>
> 13 — But behold, that which is of God inviteth and enticeth to do good continually; wherefore, every thing which inviteth and enticeth to do good, and to love God, and to serve him, is inspired of God.
>
> 14 — Wherefore, take heed, my beloved brethren, that ye do not judge that which is evil to be of God, or that which is good and of God to be of the devil.

Mormon once again lays out that doctrine taught throughout the Book of Mormon: that which is good is from God, and that which is evil is from the adversary. Although that might seem to be a simple, nearly trivial assertion, it is important that we recognize that the good things in our lives do come from God, so that we will recognize His hand in our lives. Likewise, it is important to acknowledge those things that invite us to do good have been placed before us by a loving God who wants us to find our way back to Him.

> Moroni 7:19 — Wherefore, I beseech of you, brethren, that ye should search diligently in the light of Christ that ye may know good from evil; and if ye will lay hold upon

> every good thing, and condemn it not, ye certainly will be a child of Christ.
>
> 20 — And now, my brethren, how is it possible that ye can lay hold upon every good thing?
>
> 21 — And now I come to that faith, of which I said I would speak; and I will tell you the way whereby ye may lay hold on every good thing.
>
> 22 — For behold, God knowing all things, being from everlasting to everlasting, behold, he sent angels to minister unto the children of men, to make manifest concerning the coming of Christ; and in Christ there should come every good thing.

To find our way back to our Heavenly Father, we must find those good things that point us back to Him. As we learn how to judge between good and evil, we are learning how to return to God. Mormon shows us how to, as he puts it, "lay hold on every good thing," which is to seek Christ, the source of all that is good, the only path back to our Father.

> Moroni 7:37 — Behold I say unto you, Nay; for it is by faith that miracles are wrought; and it is by faith that angels appear and minister unto men; wherefore, if these things have ceased wo be unto the children of men, for it is because of unbelief, and all is vain.

Mormon's phrase "it is by faith that miracles are wrought" always brings to my mind the title of President Spencer W. Kimball's famous book, *Faith Precedes the Miracle.* President Kimball focused on faith and miracles at the individual level, teaching us that we need to cultivate our faith before expecting to see miracles in our lives. Mormon, in contrast, is focusing more on the level of the church or the society. In either case, though, the governing principle is the same. Because it is by faith that miracles are wrought, faith does indeed precede the miracle, both temporally and causally.

> Moroni 7:46 — Wherefore, my beloved brethren, if ye have not charity, ye are nothing, for charity never faileth.

> Wherefore, cleave unto charity, which is the greatest of all, for all things must fail—
>
> 47 — But charity is the pure love of Christ, and it endureth forever; and whoso is found possessed of it at the last day, it shall be well with him.
>
> 48 — Wherefore, my beloved brethren, pray unto the Father with all the energy of heart, that ye may be filled with this love, which he hath bestowed upon all who are true followers of his Son, Jesus Christ; that ye may become the sons of God; that when he shall appear we shall be like him, for we shall see him as he is; that we may have this hope; that we may be purified even as he is pure. Amen.

"Charity never faileth" is a phrase that has become something of a cliché in our society, but as we reflect on this phrase in the context of Mormon's stirring words, the original power of this phrase is restored. When Mormon writes of charity, he is not writing about the mere human inclination to do good for others; rather, he is writing about the pure love of Christ, the charity that motivated the full, final, infinite sacrifice of the Savior. To apply the Atonement in our lives, we must ourselves have charity, meaning that we must come unto Christ and take His love into our hearts as we seek to subsume our will in his.

> Moroni 8:10 — Behold I say unto you that this thing shall ye teach—repentance and baptism unto those who are accountable and capable of committing sin; yea, teach parents that they must repent and be baptized, and humble themselves as their little children, and they shall all be saved with their little children.

Here is another of those verses that I had read many times without ever giving it much thought. Perhaps because I knew that Mormon was leading up to his impassioned discussion of why little children need not be baptized, I tended to gloss over this verse, thinking that it was simply saying that we need to humble ourselves and be more like children in that respect.

But as I read this verse with fresh eyes, I suddenly saw a meaning that I had never seen before: "yea, teach parents that they must repent and be baptized, and humble themselves as their little children, and they shall all be saved with their little children." What a marvelous doctrine Mormon has given us here! Here truly is a verse that should, if nothing else, provide parents in the church with a powerful incentive to hold family home evenings.

The promise that parents can be saved with their children can be seen as a foreshadowing of the blessings of the temple, wherein parents are sealed to children so that all can be saved and exalted as eternal families. To discover such a pearl of doctrine hidden within what seemed to be a verse that could be quickly skimmed over is quite a rewarding surprise.

> Moroni 8:25 — And the first fruits of repentance is baptism; and baptism cometh by faith unto the fulfilling the commandments; and the fulfilling the commandments bringeth remission of sins;
>
> 26 — And the remission of sins bringeth meekness, and lowliness of heart; and because of meekness and lowliness of heart cometh the visitation of the Holy Ghost, which Comforter filleth with hope and perfect love, which love endureth by diligence unto prayer, until the end shall come, when all the saints shall dwell with God.

Similar to the many previous teachings in the Book of Mormon about the relationship between humility, repentance, faith, hope, and charity, Mormon here outlines the progression of those who are humble and repentant from baptism through hope, charity, and ultimately a return to our Heavenly Father. Mormon teaches of the importance of the Holy Ghost in bearing witness to the repentant, a theme that Moroni will echo in his great exhortation to those who read the Book of Mormon:

> Moroni 10:3 — Behold, I would exhort you that when ye shall read these things, if it be wisdom in God that ye should read them, that ye would remember how merciful the Lord hath been unto the children of men, from the

> creation of Adam even down until the time that ye shall receive these things, and ponder it in your hearts.
>
> 4 — And when ye shall receive these things, I would exhort you that ye would ask God, the Eternal Father, in the name of Christ, if these things are not true; and if ye shall ask with a sincere heart, with real intent, having faith in Christ, he will manifest the truth of it unto you, by the power of the Holy Ghost.
>
> 5 — And by the power of the Holy Ghost ye may know the truth of all things.

Moroni's exhortation contains Moroni's promise: those who read the Book of Mormon may ask God whether that which is taught in the book is true and then have that knowledge revealed to them along with much more. Verse 4 has particular power in that it invokes all three members of the Godhead. We are to ask God the Father in the name of Christ, and with faith in Christ. If we do this sincerely, the Holy Ghost will reveal to us the truth of all things.

> Moroni 10:20 — Wherefore, there must be faith; and if there must be faith there must also be hope; and if there must be hope there must also be charity.
>
> 21 — And except ye have charity ye can in nowise be saved in the kingdom of God; neither can ye be saved in the kingdom of God if ye have not faith; neither can ye if ye have no hope.
>
> 22 — And if ye have no hope ye must needs be in despair; and despair cometh because of iniquity.
>
> 23 — And Christ truly said unto our fathers: If ye have faith ye can do all things which are expedient unto me.
>
> 24 — And now I speak unto all the ends of the earth—that if the day cometh that the power and gifts of God shall be done away among you, it shall be because of unbelief.

As we come to the final verses of the Book of Mormon, we find for one final time a brief but impassioned discourse on the topic of faith, hope, and charity. As we read these verses, we come to see that a choice has been placed before us: we can choose to exercise faith, and through our faith and the goodness of God come to have hope and charity, or we can choose the path of unbelief, which will eventually lead us to lose hope and fall into decline and despair.

Reflecting on this choice and the contrasting kinds of life to which it may lead, we may also come to reflect on another doctrine that has been taught throughout the Book of Mormon, the doctrine of restoration. If during this life we choose to exercise the faith that will lead us to have hope and charity, then we can expect to have faith, hope, and charity in the life to come. If, on the other hand, we choose to live lives marked by unbelief, hopelessness, and despair, that is what we will have to look forward to in the life to come. It would be as though we had come to believe not what we have been taught by the Book of Mormon, but rather what we may have heard in a popular beer commercial from a few years back: "It just doesn't get any better than this." Such a thought, taken seriously, surely would lead to hopelessness and despair. How blessed we are to have the testimony of Moroni and the other inspired witnesses recorded in the Book of Mormon!

> Moroni 10:29 — And God shall show unto you, that that which I have written is true.

After testifying mightily to the fundamental truths of the gospel of Jesus Christ, Moroni reiterates his promise in no uncertain terms. As we read these words, we know that he wrote them based on the faith, hope, and charity that he possessed, qualities that sustained him through all of the unimaginably terrible experiences that he went through and the desperate temporal circumstances in which he wrote and prepared to seal up these final words:

> Moroni 10:30 — And again I would exhort you that ye would come unto Christ, and lay hold upon every good gift, and touch not the evil gift, nor the unclean thing.
>
> 31 — And awake, and arise from the dust, O Jerusalem; yea, and put on thy beautiful garments, O daughter of Zion; and strengthen thy stakes and enlarge thy borders forever, that thou mayest no more be confounded, that the

> covenants of the Eternal Father which he hath made unto thee, O house of Israel, may be fulfilled.
>
> 32 — Yea, come unto Christ, and be perfected in him, and deny yourselves of all ungodliness; and if ye shall deny yourselves of all ungodliness, and love God with all your might, mind and strength, then is his grace sufficient for you, that by his grace ye may be perfect in Christ; and if by the grace of God ye are perfect in Christ, ye can in nowise deny the power of God.
>
> 33 — And again, if ye by the grace of God are perfect in Christ, and deny not his power, then are ye sanctified in Christ by the grace of God, through the shedding of the blood of Christ, which is in the covenant of the Father unto the remission of your sins, that ye become holy, without spot.

Moroni closes the Book of Mormon with the strong exhortation that we "come unto Christ." The closing verses of the book resonate with the gospel and the doctrine of Christ. As Moroni exhorts us, we must "lay hold upon" and firmly embrace that which is good and "touch not the evil gift, nor the unclean thing."

Once more our choice in life has been laid out clearly before us. We can choose light, life, and beauty through Christ, or we can "be confounded."

Once again we are shown the deep harmony that exists between faith and works, as Moroni tells us that if we love and serve God with all our heart, mind, and strength, then will His grace be sufficient for us that we may be "perfect in Christ." Our sins can be remitted and we can "become holy, without spot."

> Moroni 10:34 — And now I bid unto all, farewell. I soon go to rest in the paradise of God, until my spirit and body shall again reunite, and I am brought forth triumphant through the air, to meet you before the pleasing bar of the great Jehovah, the Eternal Judge of both quick and dead. Amen.

In the final verse of the Book of Mormon, Moroni bids us farewell.

Little did he apparently know that he would in a future time be among men again, shepherding the young Joseph Smith. The record he had sealed away would be exhumed from the dust to be translated by the gift and power of God, the record that we have just read in response to the challenge of that beloved twenty-first-century prophet, President Gordon B. Hinckley.

Epilogue: President Hinckley's Promise

While reading the Book of Mormon in response to the challenge issued by President Hinckley—indeed, while reading it several times and pondering it carefully in preparation for teaching it—I truly did gain a greater appreciation for the doctrines that it contains. No other book teaches so forcefully about the Atonement of Jesus Christ. No other book witnesses so powerfully of the Savior.

As we read the Book of Mormon again, we are reminded of the necessity and the power of repentance. We read about individuals and entire nations who have strayed from the strait and narrow path but are forgiven as they humbly seek to return. In some instances, such as the conversion of Alma, we see the mercy of the Lord manifested in an extraordinary angelic intervention. Even in that account, however, we see the Lord allowed Alma to make the choice to repent for himself. The Lord may have forced the issue, but He did not decide the issue.

In the Book of Mormon, we encounter the phrase "baptized unto repentance." This should be a powerful reminder to us of the importance of humility in our lives. We often hear and say that baptism is the gate into the celestial kingdom, but without repentance, our mortal journey will not take us to that destination. We are often taught as members of the Church that when we partake of the sacrament, we renew our baptismal covenant. We must also renew our desire to repent. We must be repentant to partake of the sacrament worthily, and if we partake of the sacrament worthily, we should covenant to remain repentant. The Book of Mormon testifies of the fundamental relationship between baptism and repentance, and how they both stem from and lead to faith in Christ.

The Book of Mormon also repeatedly and lovingly teaches how faith in Christ leads us to hope, which hope leads us to charity, which charity is the pure love of Christ. As we exercise faith in Christ and seek to do His will, we gain through the Spirit a portion of His pure love, enabling us to press forward through this life with love for God and for all our brothers and sisters.

Yes, the Book of Mormon also teaches that there is opposition in all things, but if we do not let ourselves be overcome by despair, then we can have hope that the good things we have been blessed with in this life will be restored to us in the life to come. We learn from the Book of Mormon that life is not lived in vain. Although this mortal life is a trial and a probationary time, it is also a time for us to prepare to live in eternity with our Father in Heaven if we learn to apply the Atonement in our lives.

Throughout the pages of the Book of Mormon, we read of the role of the Savior in enabling men and women to be saved. We read of His power, His mercy, His wisdom, His patience, His glory, His condescension, His teaching, His suffering, His resurrection, and His matchless love for all humankind—and for each of us as individuals.

In reading the Book of Mormon in response to President Hinckley's challenge, I developed a fuller and deeper testimony of the Savior. I came to understand more profoundly the need to live humbly and repentantly. I came to appreciate more gratefully the emblems of the sacrament and the ordinances of the temple, all of which point to Christ, as does the Book of Mormon.

Indeed, as I read and reflected on the Book of Mormon in response to President Hinckley's challenge, I came to realize what our late leader had prophetically envisioned when he issued that challenge: "Without reservation I promise you that if each of you will observe this simple program, regardless of how many times you previously may have read the Book of Mormon, there will come into your homes an added measure of the Spirit of the Lord, a strengthened resolution to walk in obedience to His commandments, and a stronger testimony of the living reality of the Son of God."[1]

I have attempted in this book to communicate and celebrate some of the truth and beauty found in the Book of Mormon. More precisely, I should say that I have attempted to communicate some of the truths and beautiful things that I have found in the Book of Mormon. My hope is that I have whetted your appetite to read the Book of Mormon for yourself—no matter how many times you may have read it previously—so you will find more of these true and beautiful things for yourself. If you do so, you will come to realize as I did the full measure of President Hinckley's—and Moroni's—promise.

NOTE

1. Gordon B. Hinckley, "First Presidency Message: A Testimony Vibrant and True," *Ensign,* Aug. 2005, 3.

About the Author

Karl Nehring converted to The Church of Jesus Christ of Latter-day Saints as a teenager. He graduated in 1977 from BYU with a BA in two majors: communications (journalism emphasis) and philosophy. In 1981, he received an MA in philosophy from Ohio State University, after which he completed several more years of graduate study in communication (emphasis on rhetoric and argumentation). For more than twenty years, he has enjoyed a career in environmental restoration at Battelle Memorial Institute in Columbus, Ohio. His church callings have included high councilor, bishop, bishop's counselor, Gospel Doctrine teacher, and temple ordinance worker. During the past few years, he has taught Institute classes both at the Columbus Ohio Institute and out among the wards in his stake. He and his wife, Marilyn, are the parents of seven children.

0 26575 52460 4